INTELLECTUAL STRIPPER

Sustainable Networking
For a World Without Barriers

Irene Magistro

Copyright © 2022 Irene Magistro

All rights reserved.

ISBN: 9798398831047

Thanks to my Father, who taught me the value of personal connection. The importance of active listening and showing appreciation. Asking anyone who talks to me for their name because we are all human beings, and we all appreciate being known for who we are, and it all starts with the name.

Thanks to Roberta, who guided me in using words and supported me with the love of a sister.

Thanks to my son Antonio, my source of inspiration, always.

CONTENTS

FOREWORD 1
WARNINGS 3
WHY 5
FROM THE BEGINNING 7
CHANGE 10
NETWORKING 15
    #Networking is NOT sales, and it is NOT marketing 16
    #Your network should not serve as a mailing list. 18
    #Networking is not a job placement office 19
    #Networking is not EVIL 20
WHAT IS THE VALUE OF NETWORKING 21
    #PLANET AND PEOPLE. AND PURPOSE 24
    #PROFIT 26
UPGRADE OR DOWNGRADE 29
MINDSET 32
WE ALL CHANGE, WE ALWAYS CHANGE 35
LEARN TO UNLEARN 37
    #SATISFACTION 37
    #FRUSTRATION 39
FEAR 42
    #STORY OF A REQUEST 44
All you need is... NET 49
    #THINK OUT OF THE BOX 51

- #THE PERFECTION TRAP ... 52
- #21 DAYS ... 53
- * ... 55
- WE ALWAYS COPY. WE COPY EVERYONE ... 58
- WE ALWAYS LIE. WE ALL LIE ... 63
  - #THE MIND LIES ... 67
  - #FROM BIASES TO ERRORS ... 70
- * ... 73
- TAME - DOMESTICATE ... 75
  - #1. 'P' FOR PACING ... 76
  - #2. 'P' FOR PRACTICE, PERPETUATION ... 78
  - #3. 'P' FOR PLEASURE ... 79
  - #4. THE PLEASURE 'P' ... 82
- TRAIN ... 84
- COACHING ... 86
- GET RID OF… ... 88
  - #1. LABELS ... 88
  - #2. FEAR OF BEING REJECTED ... 90
  - #3. COLLECTION OF CONTACTS ... 91
  - #4. ILLUSION OF TALENT ... 91
  - #5. MIND-READERS ... 92
- GET USED TO… ... 94
  - #1. EMPATHY ... 94
  - #2. ACTIVE LISTENING ... 95

#3. PREPARATION	98
#4. ASSERTIVE	99
#5. CARE	101
#6. FUN	102
About the Author	103
End Credits	105

FOREWORD

By **Mindy Gibbins-Klein**

Irene Magistro is a warm, intelligent, and highly talented business professional who cares about all business leaders and entrepreneurs but especially women. I first met her at a business meeting I was running in New York, and she had flown over from Italy to be part of it. I quickly realized that this was one exceptional entrepreneur! What impressed me most was the way she instantly bonded with the other professional women in the room, got involved in the conversations, and looked to help others. We soon became good friends as well as colleagues.

Her insights in social issues, human nature, and leadership impressed me from the first moment I met her, and she continues to expand on her ideas and goals to help more professional women achieve their potential. Never one to rest on her laurels, Irene is always looking for the next challenge, a great example being the movement she is creating.

This book is about human connection, one of the most important values we all share. When we meet someone, we really connect with, we see the potential in them as well as the potential within ourselves. When we feel disconnected, we miss out on the best way to live life and do business. In this age of uncertainty and fear, it can be challenging to find the right people and create a supportive network for yourself, but that is what you must do.

Networking with other clever women is essential for business and career growth. You will meet hundreds or even thousands of people in your business life, and it is impossible to keep them all close (nor do you want to!) The key is to find clever women, learn from them, share with them, and grow with them. Once you connect with one clever woman, you will find more because they know how to find the best people.

Finding the best people to connect with can be tricky, especially in a virtual world. In my business career, I have always focused on finding the most interesting and positive friends and role models, so I can keep my own spirits up and focus on continuous personal development. Whenever I have experienced a challenge, I have gone to my network and found love, support, and encouragement to keep going and try new approaches.

Irene Magistro is one of those people I will always admire and someone I can confide in to get that encouragement and support. I am delighted to see this important book being released and her wisdom being shared with the world. She has also collected stories from women who will amaze, delight and inspire you to do more and to be more.

Trust the concepts and ideas in this book, and then trust yourself to follow in the path of the amazing women who have gone before. Take action and become an even better role model for the women around you and for the next generation. And have fun doing it!

Mindy Gibbins-Klein
Founder of The Book Midwife® and author of The Thoughtful Leader

WARNINGS

Dear reader, I invite you to embark on a transformative journey where we explore the evolution of the mindset of a networker. This fresh and vibrant viewpoint goes beyond conventional strategies and delves into the core of who you are.

Through anecdotes, reflections, and practical insights, we will explore how your authenticity, curiosity, and empathy can become powerful catalysts in nurturing a valuable professional network that spans a lifetime.

As we embark on this journey together, I draw upon my own experiences and cultural heritage to provide a unique lens through which to view networking. Growing up in Italy, a country renowned for its rich social fabric, I have witnessed firsthand the art of forging genuine connections. Italians understand networking is not a mechanical process but an organic interplay of emotions, trust, and shared values. By embracing this mindset, we can cultivate relationships that extend far beyond the realm of business transactions, creating bonds rooted in mutual respect, reciprocity, and long-term collaboration.

This introduction is necessary to prepare you to challenge the traditional notions of networking and embark on a voyage of self-discovery and connection. Let us uncover the immense value of embracing networking as an integral part of your life.

In this book, we will delve into the principles that underpin successful networking and discover how they intersect with the Italian way of life, my way of life. By integrating these insights into your personal and professional journey, you will acquire the tools to build a resilient and authentic network that will support you throughout your career and beyond.

Together, we will explore the profound truth that networking starts from within, and by nurturing your own growth and embracing the world with an open heart, you will unlock the limitless potential of building a valuable professional network for life.

WHY

Why "intellectual stripper"?

I chose the title "Intellectual Stripper" to provoke curiosity and challenge conventional thinking.

The term "stripper" evokes images of removing layers, exposing oneself, and embracing vulnerability. Similarly, in the context of networking, it refers to stripping away the barriers that hinder genuine connections and inhibiting personal growth.

Why strip ourselves of the layers we have on, inside, and even around us? Because these layers often act as shields, preventing us from truly connecting with others on a deeper level. By removing them, we can engage authentically and form meaningful relationships.

Why domesticate ourselves to openness? We become receptive to new ideas, perspectives, and experiences by cultivating openness. This willingness to embrace diversity and engage in dialogue enables us to broaden our horizons and expand our understanding of the world.

Why train ourselves to build sustainable and valuable connections? Sustainable connections are those that go beyond superficial interactions and contribute to personal and professional growth. By investing time and effort in building such relationships, we can create a network of support, collaboration, and mutual benefit.

Why learn to connect with people, empathize with them, and listen to them? Human connection lies at the heart of successful networking. Through genuine empathy and active listening, we can develop a deeper understanding of others' needs, aspirations, and challenges. This understanding allows us to provide meaningful support and forge long-lasting connections.

Why learn to give—to people, the land, and the planet? Sustainable networking involves a sense of responsibility towards others and the world. By giving back, whether through mentorship, environmental stewardship, or social impact initiatives, we contribute to a better future for ourselves and future generations.

In conclusion, the reason for the subtitle "Sustainable networking for a world without barriers" is rooted in the fragility and ever-changing nature of our lives. We must adapt to evolving contexts and the needs of the people within them.

Networking offers an extraordinary opportunity to open doors we never imagined, and by stripping away our preconceptions and embracing sustainability, we can foster positive change in our lives and the world.

"Intellectual Stripper" speaks to the masks and conditioning we carry, as well as the importance of giving and supporting one another. By exposing our vulnerabilities and working together, we can improve not only our own circumstances but also those of future generations. Networking becomes a powerful tool in this journey, enabling us to connect, collaborate, and create a world without barriers.

FROM THE BEGINNING

I was born in Sicily, and until the age of eight, I grew up in the same city where historical figures like Archimedes and Paul of Tarsus once lived, near the historic walls of Ortigia, transformed into a fortified island by the Spaniards.

I have always been inquisitive, even from a very young age, so much so that even before kindergarten, I had learned to read independently. One day I was in my father's Ford Taunus, and we passed by a billboard; I read what was written on it and told him. He couldn't believe it.

"How do you know that?"
"I read it."
"You read it?"
"I read it."

I was four years old, hadn't even started kindergarten yet, and had learned to read without anyone teaching me. The following year, my mother enrolled me in the Ursuline Sisters' school, where I was incredibly bored. I don't think my restlessness was due to the rules or the monastic order (I was too young to realize that), but I didn't like being there. So one day, my mother came to pick me up and, talking to my teacher Adriana, who had the same name as her, she decided to change my school. I had just turned five and was too young for first grade. Back then, the regulations for handling exceptional cases like mine were unclear. We were always at the mercy of a new educational reform. Nothing has changed today.

So, my mother pulled some strings and spoke to various principals, and finally found an elementary school with the excellent teacher De Agostini, who welcomed me and guided me in my growth until the fourth grade. I loved the new school very much, with one downside: mathematics. I don't even call it mathematics, but "numbers" because it causes me so much discomfort. For me, addition is a drama, and subtraction is a disaster.

This aversion to "numbers" has been with me forever, but I hadn't noticed it until my mother pointed it out, reminding me that, as a child, I used to cover pages of poorly written and erased numbers with my hand. I don't remember it, but even the act of repression says a lot about me: on the one hand, about my desire to do homework well, and on the other, about how much I feared the judgment of others.

Over the years, I have built a kind of armor, a protective garment to defend myself.

Not everyone understands that sometimes, a person needs extra protection—not just because they fear for their own suffering and disappointment, but also because they worry about the impact they may have on others. I have been told that my tongue is sharper than a knife. I don't like to think that my words can hurt others. I wouldn't want to be hurt.

I have worked hard on myself to direct my communication skills toward safe and generative grounds of positive reactions or, in any case, predictable and manageable ones.

Communication is everything; it is the foundation of everything. Clear communication skills are essential to maintain balance in all interpersonal relationships.

"In today's society, aptly defined as the society of communication," - Vera Gheno writes - in "Potere alle parole[1]" "everyone's life is full of situations that require the use of language, and using it well is preferable. Working, having a romantic relationship, shopping, traveling, seeking medical care, being on social networks, raising children, participating in a debate, obtaining a document from a public administration, defending oneself from an accusation, communicating a discovery to others, studying, teaching, going to the cinema—these are all daily tasks for which it would be beneficial to use to the best of our abilities that incredible toolbox with which we were equipped at birth."

---

[1] Vera Gheno has a Sociolinguistics degree and a Ph.D. in Italian Linguistics. She teaches at the University of Florence, deals with translations, sexism, and the inclusiveness of the Italian language, and writes beautiful books, including "Power to Words. Why use them better", published by Einaudi in 2019.

Unfortunately, using this "toolbox" well is not easy to achieve because while you are on the communicative path, you cannot see where you are going, and sometimes you may crash into a wall.

Through practice, technique, study, and facing walls, I have learned to look beyond the tip of my nose and ask myself in advance, "What do you want to achieve from this exchange? What consequence do you expect if you use these words instead of those?"

One must be very careful.

That's how, at the age of eighteen, I embarrassed myself in front of an old family friend, someone I had grown up with, a little older than me, and for whom I had always had a crush.

A more-than-casual kiss happened.

It confused me greatly. Perhaps I misunderstood an attitude. I was very inexperienced and also very infatuated. I have a passionate nature; add to that the young age, eighteen years thirty years ago, and you wrote a fiery letter on paper with ink that still haunts me with embarrassment today.

In the good old times of letters sent with stamps, "verba volant, scripta manet" (tr. spoken words fly away, written words remain) was a permanent seal on your foolish musings. So there is a letter somewhere in the world that highlights how silly I was at eighteen, in love with someone who didn't care about me at all.

That embarrassment would never happen today with the safety and control I have sewn into myself.

It wasn't the only time I took up pen and paper to assertively express my thoughts and disagreements.

A friend stopped talking to me for a few years.

A boyfriend left me.

Lesson learned: Dance like nobody's watching, but write your messages, emails, and letters as if they'll be read in court.

CHANGE

At the age of eight, everything changes.

My parents decide, out of the blue, to leave Sicily and buy a pharmacy in Calabria. But we don't move to Reggio or Tropea. Instead, we go from the cradle of Mediterranean civilization to live in a remote mountain village called Mesoraca.

Mesoraca is at the foot of Mount Giove, in the Sila Piccola, on the slopes of Mount Femminamorta. And it's cold. It's February, and I see snow for the first time.

It's a world away from Syracuse: just four thousand residents, no washing machines, a new dialect, and a whole different vibe. The streets are empty, and it's freezing.

We stand in front of a tall, weathered wooden door. The lock is opened with an old-fashioned, oversized key that could easily serve as a keychain.

We pass through the entrance and find ourselves in a dark hallway, with plaster peeling off the walls and a series of black iron rings attached. I ask what the rings are used for, and I'm told they're for tying horses.

Horses inside a house?

So it seems.

The right arch looks like a cave, and from there, there is a small door that leads to the basement of the house, where I am told that food (meat, cured meats, sausages, hams, aged cheeses, and dried vegetables) used to be stored.

In front of us is a large staircase with cement steps, around which the entire house is built. On the wall, there are two holes at the ends of a slit, closed with cement but still visible. What are they for? I ask.

I will discover they are makeshift gun sights, aiming at the door and shooting at wrongdoers from inside the house.

Shoot?

"Shoot, but without leaving the house. We're in Calabria, which was bandit country in the late 1800s," says the old pharmacist who's serving as our guide and will stay with us for another six months.

The staircase stops at a landing from which another steep staircase on the right leads up, or you can go to the main entrance on the left.

The old pharmacist is an older man, famous for his stinginess, like Scrooge, and he shows us the house without turning on the lights.

Candles are better, it seems.

I count seventeen rooms, a large hall for parties, an entryway with a ceiling over thirteen feet high, and thick walls made of river stones.

During the tour, he tells us that the old lords of Mesoraca built the house and that Princess Caracciolo also lived there.

"In the old hidden garden," he says, "the one overlooking the cliff that leads to the river, the princess was beheaded."

Things keep getting better. But the surprises are not over: there is no central heating here, the house has no heating, only a fireplace in the dining room on the lower floor. Upstairs, there are rooms without fireplaces and windows recycled from old doors that let in drafts.

We sleep with six blankets, all in the same bed (except the pharmacist!).

Of the two streams in Mesoraca, one flows beneath our house: the riverbed is at the foot of the "timpa," a cliff above which our dwelling is situated. No car noise can be heard, nothing at all: the silence is constant, day and night. When it rains, the stream swells and becomes dark, extremely frightening. When it doesn't rain, or before it does, fog covers everything, and when it snows, it's not the same snow as in the movies, with calm flakes falling from the sky, but a storm of wind freezes the face.

Upon seeing the town square for the first time, my mother turned pale. If I had been in her place, with the eyes of then but perhaps also the eyes of today, I would have quickly jumped into the car to return home, to Sicily, to Via Polibio number 82, in my fortified and bustling Syracuse, full of people, colors, scents, and laughter. There is no one around or almost no one, but there are chickens and hens on the street, scratching outside the houses, and donkeys waiting for someone to load them and use them to climb the mountains to gather olives or chestnuts.

Our house doesn't have a washing machine. After a while, we discover that nobody has one in Mesoraca: women go to wash clothes at the river, carrying baskets on their heads with the laundry that they then beat against the limestone rocks.

To reach the town, there are two bridges, the only access and escape route, and when one of them is closed, everyone is afraid of being isolated.

Here, I find that lineage is even more important than in Syracuse; people meet you and ask, "Who's your family?" They ask to know which family and lineage you belong to. A significant portion of the inhabitants has a nickname that says something about them, like Mico Sciallino, the butcher, a tall man who looks like an Ottoman figure from a textbook, whom I mention because I have much affection for him, so much so that I consider him like an uncle.

Since one of his ancestors was known for always wearing a shawl—earning the nickname "Sciallino"—he goes by the same name.

Living in a small town has its pros and cons. People are welcoming, but the closeness they create is only sometimes sincere. In the inland areas, Calabria in the late 1980s was greatly influenced by medieval legacies and social class divisions, often based on land ownership.

The house where I grew up, a large mansion from the late 1600s divided into four sections, assigned to as many families, had attic sections (lofts) or remote corners of the house intended for the servants. When it was our time to live in that house, we inherited the daughter of one of the palace servants, who came to help my mother manage the household three times a week.

In the past, helping with household tasks was rewarded with room and board and inclusion in the family. In our day, it's compensated with money.

The ancient late 19th-century registry records, the ones still handwritten, are kept in the municipalities, and you can read "family status of -surname-" starting from the head of the family down to the last of the servants, listed as part of it.

With this legacy, the mentality of the place is strongly influenced by belonging to a specific social class. They were no longer closed classes, but the union between a socially mixed couple always caused a stir in the town.

People felt authorized to communicate it to the family as a defender of the maiden's purity or the boy's honor.

One day, I was on the side of the road, riding my scooter, and I was having a chat with a boy slightly older than me (I was sixteen). A lady passing by literally ran to the pharmacy and whispered to my mother's ear that she had seen me.

"I know," my mother said to close the discussion.

Until the late '90s, couples couldn't even hold hands; girls wouldn't get in cars with their friends, and if they did, they'd lie down in the backseat until they were out of sight.

Needless to say, all these rules never belonged to me. I was the only girl in Calabria to own a scooter in the 1980s, and the same was when I got my first Honda 125F.

I never understood being judgmental.

I don't like to judge. In the end, why do it?

I don't see the usefulness.

For example, this way of communicating doesn't produce positive results.

I am unconsciously permeated by Socrates' philosophy of the three sieves.

One of his disciples rushes to Socrates to inform him that one of his friends is speaking ill of him. Socrates tells him to calm down and, before saying anything else, asks him to examine the message through the three filters, the three sieves.

One: "Are you certain that what you are about to say is true?"

The disciple thinks about it and concludes that he has no solid evidence and that it could simply be an assessment from a different perspective.

- Does what you want to say have a positive content?
- No.
- What you are about to say, you don't know if it's true, but you know it will hurt - Socrates concludes, moving on to the third and final sieve.
- Will what you're about to tell me about my friend be helpful to me in any way?

The disciple hesitates.

- I don't think so - he answers - I believe what I'm about to tell you will distance you from your friend.

- If what you want to tell me is not helpful, positive, or true, why should I want to hear it?

This story summarizes my relationship with hearsay news, gossip, and rumors.

Unfortunately, Mesoraca, where I spent so much time, has always been filled with village bulletins that are often false, not for good, or useful

NETWORKING

The term "networking" comes from the idea of a "net" of interconnected points or nodes.
Therefore, networking involves operating within and through multiple networks: one that originated from the early ARPAnet experiments (the precursor to the internet) and another that we have to build and interconnect. Yet, the first images that come to mind when we think of networking are not the nodes of the network or the connections from one country to another. They are not even the bonds between people.
Although Google currently shows half a billion results for the term "networking" and over 21 million for "books on networking," our understanding of networking remains unclear and somewhat ambiguous.
In a situation where a company's revenue is falling, and the client base is shrinking, board members may start discussing the need for networking to boost sales and attract new clients.

- Okay, but how?

One of the higher-ups posts something on LinkedIn and, while awaiting likes and comments, reviews our profiles, shakes their head, and advises us to start networking.

- Why should we invest time, which is already scarce, in something that may not seem that important? How will building relationships actually boost our productivity?

The fact is that, without a doubt, it does increase productivity and foster connections.

Networking is essential; everyone knows that, but isn't it too late? And most importantly: how do we do it?

Despite the overwhelming number of concepts taught in universities and post-graduate courses, none really teach us how to create, nurture, and leverage a relationship network.

We are bombarded with messages and press releases that extol the power of connections, but the volume of information is so large and varied that the result is a big mess.

Specifically, the problem is that we don't really understand what it means to network effectively.

Sure, we're familiar with the term, but what we really need is a concrete strategy for putting it into practice. How do we start networking? And when?

> "Networking is probably one of the most misunderstood skills that today's workforce needs for career and business success.[2]"

Before reflecting together on what it is and how to support it, let's start by excluding what networking is not:
1. It is not sales, and it is not marketing.
2. It is not HR – a job placement office.
3. It is not evil.

#Networking is NOT sales, and it is NOT marketing

While it's true that sales can benefit from networking and that marketing involves relationships, networking itself is not a direct mechanism for increasing revenue or followers.

---

[2] Financial Times Guides - "Business Networking: how to use the power of online and offline Networking for Business Success" - " second edition, Heather Townsend

"A common mistake is viewing networking as the initial step in the sales process." Effective networking is not about selling or asking for a new job; it's about developing strong relationships where work and opportunities will come through, not from!"[3]

If we network to sell (a product, an experience, ourselves), the only thing we almost certainly achieve is damage to our credibility. That's why networking doesn't help increase market share, especially if the word networking makes us think of pyramid business models in multilevel marketing and the mythology of Tupperware and similar things.

NETWORK + MARKETING

Do we remember when we were invited to an event that would change our lives (and if it hasn't happened to us, it has undoubtedly happened to someone we know), or who promises on social media and WhatsApp a financial freedom never experienced before and incremental earnings based on word of mouth? The invitation to join a "big family" where the more time you dedicate to building connections, the more you earn, like Pietro, who managed to make 15,000 euros in a month! We almost believe it, but logic prevails; networking leaves a bitter taste in our mouths, and just thinking about it makes us step back. We see the deception, and the **network becomes a trap** like trawling or butterfly nets.

Networking should not be equated with a marketing department. Those who network are interested in something other than sharing their contacts to promote our brand, our new consulting company, or to help us sell this or that product/service. Of course, they know many people and could open many doors for us, but they may not do it, may not want to, or may not be able to do it. Certainly, someone with many contacts who is naturally a networker, if they are impressed by what we do, sell, and produce, will create a connection because that's how it works. What we must not do is expect it to happen.

Those who already live on connections, meaning we do nothing but build relationships, are often asked to work together. Some time ago, Marco called me and asked me to introduce him to someone who

---

[3] Financial Times Guides

might need his skills. Since Marco is a professional I have always respected, I opened a door for him and introduced him to Pietro. So far, so good, except that shortly after, Pietro returned to me and said that even though he thanked me for the connection, he would prefer to work with me rather than with Marco. The spontaneous question arises: why?

To understand what went wrong, I asked him to tell me about the meeting, and listening to him, I understood that Marco's communication needed to be more *transitional*—the transition between the primary contact, Irene, and the new contact, Pietro.

Marco assumed that, having had an excellent introduction, the connection was made. In these circumstances, however, we must give importance to the source of the referral. Marco did not emphasize what they had in common; it would have been enough to say, "How do you know Irene?" and use this "common ground" to initiate an empathetic relationship. Instead, focusing on his skills and services, like a menu in a pizzeria but in PowerPoint presentation format, he missed an opportunity. The answer to our question is that an important piece was missing in building a connection: empathy.

We must consider modifying our usual approach when we find ourselves in the replacement phase within a trust-based relationship that could bring business or generate referrals. We need to listen to the needs of the person in front of us and use their requirements to build our new approach.

If we want to "utilize" someone else's networking power, we must also let ourselves be guided and let go of control; otherwise, the contact that could have resulted in something valuable in our lives will back away.

On the other hand, when we bridge the gap between a potential client connection and a potential supplier connection, what we are buying is no longer just the product or service but the relationships behind it, its universe of values—we also believe the personal relationship of the person we trust.

#Your Network should not serve as a Mailing List.
It should not be used as a direct marketing tool, mainly because direct marketing is outdated and ineffective. Well, almost.

When we receive calls from call centers, our reaction is adverse. We are bored and annoyed; even if the person on the other end of the line may have something interesting to tell us, our predisposition is still negative.

The network needs to be nurtured like a plant.

We can maintain and grow a valuable network if we have the patience to sow and care for our plant over time and without stress. The plant that is expected to be highly fruitful will eventually stop bearing fruit.

#Networking is not a job placement office

Neither our own cultivated network nor anyone else's should serve as a job placement office. Some people believe that because we know a lot of entrepreneurs and professionals, it will be easy for us to introduce or find them a new job. But every time we connect two people, we must carefully consider who these people are and what they can do for each other and thus together for everyone else.

Similarly, if we are looking for a new occupation, before asking someone to connect us with someone else, we must look for a hook and give before asking. We should provide before even thinking of asking, remembering that even the person who could be our intermediary surely needs something (another contact or a different kind of support).

"Networking" is a phrase that is often whispered quietly. [...] Building a network has acquired a bad reputation: it is seen as a privilege of the few, as the tool with which selfish individuals pursue their own goals at the expense of others. Yet, building a network is the oldest thing we know how to do. It has made us so powerful and enduring, despite our mortality and our bodies being covered with such thin skin that a piece of wood cut at the right angle is enough to puncture it to death."[4]

---

[4] "Go: close your eyes and look at your future" - by Giancarlo Orsini, manager, and science communicator, a leading figure in the field of education who, combining work with a great passion for innovation and technology, has created a seminar that it led him to meet over 50,000 people across the country.

#Networking is not EVIL

Regardless of the clichés and misunderstandings that circulate in our heads and on our screens, the network is not wrong. At most, what is wrong is the way we use it every time we believe we can exploit it (without giving anything in return).

> *"Connecting intelligence is an adventure that is not only essential for any human being who wants to live a life worthy of the name but also the main path through which our success with the great challenges that await us will pass. Networks are wrong when they exclude someone for who they are: their skin color or sexual orientation, or when they aim to exclude someone else from something. That is evil."*[5]

We cannot ask without giving. Building a network is based on mutual relationship care. So let us never forget to ask those we want to keep active in our network: "How can I help you?"

If we don't do that, what happens? If we don't nurture our network, we are exploiting it.

Consider the implications of the word "exploit." Actions like taking, stripping, plundering, and impoverishing are the antithesis of cultivation, nurturing, growth, and well-being. In one word: sustainability.

---

[5] "Go: close your eyes and look at your future" - by Giancarlo Orsini

WHAT IS THE VALUE OF NETWORKING

A network is made up of nodes, and before machines arrived, the nodes were hand-knotted by sailors to tie the boat to the anchor, secure ropes, and even build hammocks for sleeping and shelters for protection. But even before the knots in the sea and the woods, the connection with other human beings - the construction of a network of people, communities, and clans - allowed us to survive. Until twelve thousand years ago, humans lived by gathering and hunting; for both, they needed not to be alone. In a group, opportunities increase, and dangers decrease.

The age-old saying "unity is strength" has ancient origins, and its relevance extends not just to human communities but also to biology. Specifically, it applies to cells, the fundamental units of life in all organisms, including organizations composed of people.

Literally, *networking* is a job of creating connections and mutually beneficial relationships for all elements involved.

Today, the purpose of networking is to improve our visibility or "profile," create new opportunities like jobs or contacts, find solutions and tools, and build and sustain a community.

Building and nurturing an excellent network for better visibility is akin to advertising in its truest sense, which is to make something publicly known.

We've opened a well-stocked store filled with items that people need, all of high quality, and so on. There's one problem: nobody comes to our beautiful store (and therefore, nobody buys our beautiful things), and nobody even looks for us. Yet, we are sure that our products will fly off the shelves... Yet, we have a sign and a shop window... What is the problem? Until someone knows how to find us, they cannot reach us, and as long as no one talks about us, nobody knows we exist. In this analogy that applies to both people and boutiques and online stores, we lack road signage, a series of metaphorical and actual signs.

The oldest form of advertising is the drum, also known as a tam-tam.

In the vast expanse of the internet, which is much like a forest, we need something to bridge the distance between us and those far away: a drum, or metaphorically, a strong signal. We need a tam-tam that resonates through the jungle, rises above the background noise, and brings us closer to those we want to reach.

Networking helps us build our tam-tam and ensures that word-of-mouth generates new opportunities and, thus, new possibilities. I use the term "possibilities" cautiously because it's not guaranteed that these opportunities will be immediately useful to us. We may not need another job (when we're doing well, we don't feel like changing) or to increase our market share (incredibly, not everyone wants to sell more). Yet, they might be helpful to us in the future... Or we might need answers, information, or tools. Maybe a guide. We might feel the need for a mentor, someone to help us find our way, to support us as we learn to walk that path... We might need to build a group to spread a thought or a set of ideas to help someone or defend ourselves from something.

A living network has always been used to build security, nourish its members, protect them from threats, and allow growth, evolution, and improvement, increasing well-being.

The ideas of building, nourishing, and protecting all boil down to one fundamental concept: **offering support**. This means taking tangible steps that improve our current environment.

What exactly constitutes our environment? Which specific environment are we referring to?

First and foremost, the environment is about context, which once again relates back to networking. Does that make sense? Look at the origin of this term to discover that it comes from the Latin word *contextum* - connection, bond - which is derived from the verb *contexĕre*, 'to interweave.'

The *environment* is the **context** in which we move, the specific moment, in a specific place, within specific relationships between distinct human beings that function in an equally specific way.

"Interesting, but how do you choose what to say when you create a connection?"

Whenever I am asked this question, the first answer is always, "It depends," and the second is:

There's no right content without context.

No formula works for everyone and everywhere. There is no right content, no perfect one, without considering the context, without first pausing to think about the environment we are about to enter, the type of person we are about to communicate with, the moment we both are experiencing, what matters to us and to the other person.

Context is the territory in which we move; therefore, it is also the physical environment, made up of land, trees, pollution, noise, oceans, and rising temperatures. It is the territory made up of numbers, slogans, posters, PowerPoint slides, documentaries, movies, and TV series that, on the one hand, tells us to think about the future of the planet and, on the other hand, compel us to buy another pair of shoes, another car, another house. It's the space we need to "**protect**" and "**sustain**" for both ourselves and future generations.

"It is worse, much worse than you think."
(David Wallace Wells)

It is our planet racing towards the sixth mass extinction, as David Wallace Wells, an American journalist, deputy editor of the New York Magazine, and editor at The Guardian, writes in the introduction of his book "The Uninhabitable Earth."[6] The situation on the planet is much more severe than we can imagine.

"It is worse, much worse than you think. The slowness of climate change is a fairy tale, perhaps as dangerous as the lie that tells us it is not happening at all, and it is offered to us together with several other comforting illusions: that global warming is an Arctic saga unfolding in remote places; that it is a problem that concerns only sea levels and coastal areas, not a global crisis that will spare no place and leave no form of life unchanged; that it is a crisis of the 'natural' world, not the human world; that these are two separate things, and that today we live somehow outside or beyond them, or we are protected from them, and not inevitably connected to and completely overwhelmed by them;

---

[6] "The Uninhabitable Earth", David Wallace Wells, Penguin, January 2019 – Italian edition "La Terra inabitabile", Mondadori (2020).

that wealth can be a shield against the devastation of global warming; that burning fossil fuels is the price we pay for continuous economic growth; that growth and the technology it produces will inevitably enable us to devise an escape from the environmental disaster; that in the long history of humanity, there have been other cases of threats similar in size or scope, so we can be confident in our ability to overcome them. None of this is true."

#PLANET AND PEOPLE. AND PURPOSE

Whenever we talk about the context (environment and planet), we talk about people. When we talk about people, we can only talk about purpose, which in Italian can be translated as "scope," but it's not limited to just being a goal or an objective.

PEOPLE -> PURPOSE

The word "purpose" comes from Old French "*porpose*," which in turn comes from "*porposer*," meaning "to put forward." This term is a combination of two Latin components: 'por,' meaning 'forward,' and 'pausare,' meaning 'to pause.'

It's not surprising that this trendy English term has a Latin origin. The influence of the Roman Empire on the modern world extends beyond warfare; perhaps more significantly, it includes the connections and unifications of diverse peoples who integrated and flourished together.

If we delve further into the etymology of 'purpose,' we find that it also has Greek components: 'pro,' meaning 'in front of,' and 'pausa,' meaning 'stop' or 'pause.' This suggests that the word has a complex lineage, not solely rooted in Latin.

So, "*purpose*" doesn't only come from Latin but also, and primarily, from Greek. This backward journey into a word tells us that the boundaries between humans and our stories are genuinely fluid, but it also tells us that purpose is not just a goal. It requires a pause before becoming an objective (and long before turning into a Key Performance Indicator).

It's as if it tells us to stop and put forward what we are, our essence,

rather than just a finality. Our nature, our deepest self.
So, discovering our purpose becomes something that can truly change our lives.

It's no longer tied to where we want to go, how much money we want to accumulate and/or spend, and how many things we want to have and/or show. It's something we already have, which is already within us and seeks to guide us.

More than a thing and long before a how our purpose is a why.

Why do we do what we do, no matter what, and in whatever way? Why do we get up every morning? Why do we dress the way we decide to dress? Why do we communicate? Why do we connect with the rest of the world? Why do we buy a particular product? Why do we behave in a certain way? Why do we work? And for whom are we working?

Finding our purpose serves individuals, and since it serves individuals, it serves communities of people, including companies, organizations, and publicly traded enterprises.

Moreover, finding our purpose also means getting rid of everything that goes in the opposite direction. It means freeing ourselves from mental masks that prevent us from truly being well, from all those constructions that distance us from well-being and render us incapable of providing well-being to others.

When we board an airplane, the flight attendants show us the safety procedures. The first thing to do is to put on the oxygen mask, meaning to think of ourselves before others, including those we love and travel with.

"The videomaker Destin Sandlin explained in a video why the safety instructions on commercial flights state that in case of a sudden decrease in pressure, we must always put on the oxygen mask first and then, later on, put it on the children are traveling with. To explain it, Sandlin simulated a situation of pressure decrease with the help of a team of NASA experts. He entered a room that simulated the conditions of a depressurized airplane at an altitude of 7000 meters. After about three minutes without an oxygen mask, his body started experiencing the first symptoms of "hypoxia," oxygen deficiency. He underwent a test in which he had to fit objects of geometric shapes into corresponding holes. Initially, Sandlin had no problem, but as the minutes passed, he started feeling tingling in his hands and lost the ability to distinguish between one shape and another. However, as soon as he put on the oxygen mask, he regained his cognitive abilities."[7]

So, another cornerstone of sustainability is to support ourselves (our core, our company, our organization, our territory) before being able to help someone else; to do that, our purpose needs to be a source of **profit**.

#PROFIT

As mentioned for the network to which we associate images that are not always positive, the same goes for profit: on the one hand, we are attracted to it due to storytelling that presents us with images of happy people always linked to a certain level of success, glory, and above all, wealth; on the other hand, we start looking at a profit with some suspicion.
What if there's something else? What if we're not interested in becoming billionaires? What if we don't need everything, they tell us we need?
For a few years now, several hundred professionals and managers have embraced the theory of the so-called YOLO economy, from the acronym "You Only Live Once." With the Corona-Virus 19 pandemic, the YOLOs have multiplied and continued to grow.

Something strange is happening to the exhausted, type-A millennial workers of America.

"*Something strange is happening to America's exhausted, type-A millennial workers. After a year hunched over their MacBooks, from one Zoom meeting to another, between improvised baking and marathon cycling, they turn the chessboard of their lives around and are ready to risk it all.*
Some leave comfortable and stable jobs to start a new business, turn a side gig into full-time work, or finally work on that screenplay. Others are scoffing

---

[7] https://www.ilpost.it/2016/07/27/maschera-ossigeno-aereo/

at their bosses' return-to-office mandates and threatening to quit unless they can work where and when they want. Encouraged by the increasing vaccination rate and a recovering job market, their risk appetite has grown, with their bank accounts fattened by a year of savings at home and the surge in asset prices. And while some are simply changing jobs, others are entirely abandoning the treadmill of their careers. If this movement has a battle cry, it's "YOLO" - "you only live once," an acronym popularized by rapper Drake a decade ago and since adopted by risk-loving enthusiasts. The term has become a meme among Reddit stock traders, who use it when making irresponsible bets that sometimes still pay off. More broadly, it has come to characterize the attitude that has captivated a certain type of bored employee in recent months."[8]

Brett Williams, a 33-year-old lawyer from Orlando, Florida, had his YOLO epiphany during a Zoom mediation in February, realizing that, like many of us, he was spending ten hours a day in front of the computer, feeling anything but happy.

"I thought, 'What do I have to lose? We could all die tomorrow.' So he quit, leaving his role as a partner in a large law firm to work in a smaller one and spend more time with his wife and dog. Like Brett, Olivia Messer, a former reporter for the Daily Beast, left Brooklyn and moved to Florida near her parents, where she writes as a freelancer and has plenty of time for painting and kayaking.

If "languishing" is the dominant emotion of 2021, YOLOing could be the defining trend for the workforce this year. A recent Microsoft survey found that over 40 percent of global workers considered leaving their jobs this year. Blind, an anonymous social network popular among tech workers, recently found that 49 percent of its users planned to change careers. "We've all had a year to assess whether the life we're living is the one we want," said Christina Wallace, a senior lecturer at Harvard Business School. "Especially for younger people who have been told to work hard, pay off loans, and one day you'll be able to enjoy life, but many are questioning this equation. What if they want to be happy now?"

Meanwhile, anxious about the exodus, many companies are trying to boost morale and prevent burnout. LinkedIn has given most of its employees a paid week off, while Twitter employees have been given an extra day off each month

---

[8] New York Times https://www.nytimes.com/2021/04/21/technology/welcome-to-the-yolo-economy.html

to recharge with a program called #DayofRest. Credit Suisse has given its junior bankers a $20,000 "lifestyle allowance," while Houlihan Lokey, another Wall Street firm, has provided many employees with all-inclusive vacations.

What if a week-long vacation or an extra paycheck isn't enough to make us happy? What if we want to achieve well-being and sustainability for both ourselves and our environment right now?

Therefore, first and foremost, we should understand our true nature and what we truly want for our lives (PURPOSE).

We should consider whether our **purpose** benefits not just ourselves but also our planet. This includes our immediate surroundings— PLANET— our homes, neighborhoods, cities, and countries. Finally, we should identify a coherent way to connect our purpose, the well-being of people, and the health of the planet to generating a profit. After all, discussions about sustainability are incomplete without considering the return on investment. Indeed, it may look simple on paper, and bookstores are filled with titles promising easy solutions. However, for every book or online course offering quick fixes, there are countless real-world examples of people who are far from achieving well-being or sustainability.

UPGRADE OR DOWNGRADE

> *Nothing can prevent a person with the right mental attitude from achieving their goal; nothing on Earth can help a person with the wrong mental attitude.*
> *(Thomas Jefferson)*

Why do we need to improve our lives and well-being?

According to biology, if we don't evolve, we're bound to regress. It's a fact that when a company stops growing, it stagnates. In that stagnant state, another company may acquire or outperform it, leading to its eventual decline or shutdown.

Every time a cell stops reproducing (= growing), its existence ends. Similarly, whenever humans stop moving, acting, growing, and striving to evolve, they meet the same fate as a cell or a business: they slow down, stop, and eventually die.

The drive for evolution and improvement is inherent in life (not just ours). If we have such a strong need to progress, it's fundamentally because it is linked to our survival.

Survival is not just about avoiding starvation or exposure. Fifty thousand years ago, it mostly meant not being eaten by another animal, moving around in search of food and milder temperatures, for at least two or three hundred years (only if we think about the early industrial revolutions) and at least two thousand years (if we go back to the civilizations of the Fertile Crescent), it means living above, living better, so that today is a little better than yesterday, and hopefully, tomorrow, if things go well, will be even better than today.

Literally speaking, survival is the gateway to thriving, which involves making something prosperous, fruitful, and sustainable in a way that both contributes and supports. While we recognize the importance of improving our well-being and achieving sustainability, making the necessary changes is often a challenging journey.

In his latest book, Luca Tomassini writes that ours is a new world:

"In an infinitesimal fraction of time, the landscape has changed, and with it, our habits, the rules of the game, the paradigms. As always in human history, a single event has set off a domino effect that is questioning everything we believe we know, permanently and irreversibly changing our lives. What we are experiencing today, right now, is the most drastic revolution humanity has ever witnessed. And it is the most widespread: the only one with no geographical, political, or ideological boundaries. This revolution is the only one that involves the entire planet. And it is also the fastest, so fast that it requires an adaptation that humans have never faced before. It is not a crisis; it is not a virus. It is not even a war. It is an extraordinary evolutionary leap.

To the question 'Why have we built the internet, robots, and artificial intelligence? And why, before these, have we invented and built telescopes, particle accelerators, personal computers, cars, airplanes, telephones, and cell phones?' Tomassini looks at human history, talks about survival, and later states that happiness and well-being are the driving force, sometimes unconscious, behind every action, every thought, every search, every impulse for evolution."

We are both drawn to and repelled by change, often with the same intensity. Every time we think about change, we would like it on the one hand, but on the other, we are terrified of it.

Change is a fact of life that we all have no choice but to deal with. Those of us who can acknowledge this fact and cope with change will survive. Those who can seek out change – and actively embrace it – will thrive[9].

The pace of change is accelerating and is altering the world in irreversible ways. Technological, political, and social changes are reshaping the world in ways people only begin to understand. While facing change has become more

---

[9] "Change is a fact of life that we all have no choice but to face. Those of us who are able to recognize this fact and deal with change will survive. Those who are able to seek change - and embrace it - will thrive » - The Power to Change - How to Harness Change to Make It Work for You, Campbell Macpherson

common, managing it remains challenging. Processing the intense emotions surrounding change - especially significant life-changing changes - is particularly important for successful navigation.

Campbell Macpherson identifies factors that are evident, like the internet, artificial intelligence, climate change, increased life expectancy, and the perspectives of newer generations. In his latest publication, "*The Power to Change,*" he loudly states that our mind has the power to create or block change, saying that change is difficult because human beings are wired to resist.

"Beliefs, biases, and negative thoughts are essentially self-created obstacles to block change," he says. However, we also know that as proficient as we are at creating obstacles, our minds are equally capable of removing them—much like the way a placebo can relieve pain. Kidney stones are believed to be more painful than childbirth. However, a simple 'glucose solution' of water and sugar can alleviate the pain, suggesting the mind's role in pain perception. What happened? Nothing, when we tell our brain that it can stop causing pain, it simply obeys.

A matter of *mindset*? Not only that but let's start with that.

MINDSET

> «*We either make ourselves miserable, or we
> make ourselves strong. The amount of work is the same.*»
> Carlos Castaneda

I was just born, and I don't know anything yet. After about forty weeks in a warm environment, I'm suddenly exposed to the cold. But there's no time to think about that; I have to breathe and then focus on something else, which I can't put into words yet, but I know it's crucial. As time goes by, someone will tell me that it's called surviving and that humans have particular primary and secondary needs to succeed. As days pass, I learn how to grab attention. I can't communicate yet, so for now, I send out a signal that prompts my mom to feed me or wrap me in her warm arms.

I've figured out that if I cry and my eyes get watery, she comes and fixes everything. But after a while (weeks, maybe months, I have no idea), this thing stops working, or rather, it still works, but only sometimes. So I try something new, and instead of screaming and exhausting myself, I make other sounds that make her laugh. In the meantime, I've learned to crawl to move around in the crib and then on the carpet, and here, on the floor, I've also learned to pull myself up. I discovered that if I leverage my arms and lift this huge, heavy body, I can see things a little better, not just my mom's and the other embarrassed creature's ankles, who looks at me from above and is almost afraid to touch me.

Gradually, I find that I can latch onto various things and pull myself up until I'm almost as tall as the couch. Once I manage to stay upright for a bit, I convince myself that I've got it all figured out.

I recognize the two people I see every day: one is Mom and the other is Dad, and I know this because they keep telling me. I also learn not to be scared of the elderly figures mimicking my sounds; they're my grandparents, and they're harmless.

I know I can move on my little feet, and now that I'm big, I also know that they're called feet, but if I get lost staring at something, and I'm not careful, I fall and bump into something, which really hurts, and then I cry, which in turn brings someone who picks me up.

Eventually, my small feet grow larger and more stable, and walking becomes easier. Okay, I tell myself, now I know everything there is to know: I'm big. But suddenly, after one of the countless car rides in my car seat with the tight belts, Mom drops me off in a place with many other little things that look like me and are called children. They tell me, "We are the children." And this is kindergarten. In addition to the children, there are people dressed all in black, with a dress that touches the ground, and a blanket of the same color on their heads, covering their hair.

"She's called Adriana, like me," my mom tells me, and then leaves.

I start to cry because I don't want her to leave, and I don't want to stay here.

However, she assures me that I'll have a good time and should be strong.

A minute later, I'm surrounded by children again, just a little taller, in a place where we all have to sit still and quietly in front of a table called a desk. It's the first day of elementary school, and the other children are all older than me, but the teacher knows many things and promises to teach us everything, so it's okay. I already know how to read, but unlike in kindergarten, I'm not bored at all here, and in no time, I learn how to write and remember lots of stories. I discovered the history of human beings, for example, and how they built the first tools (bowls for eating and spears for hunting). I learn about their ways of defending themselves, the first clans, and the first cities. I know grammar: here and there don't have accents, and all nine prepositions. Meanwhile, I figure out that some things are acceptable for me but not for others. Because I'm a girl, I'm expected to play with dolls, even though I prefer Playmobil and toy cars. I'm told to be gentle, act delicately, and chew with my mouth closed—things my friend doesn't have to worry about. I also learn that I should smile, but not excessively. I realize there are quite a few things I shouldn't do, or I'll get stern looks from others. I also know that certain specific things make me feel bad even if no one says anything to me, like when I can't understand numbers, and every time I see them, I get agitated, to the point that when I have to hand in a homework assignment, I lie down on the notebook and cover it, hide it, so as not to show my "horrible mistakes."

So now I know everything there is to know. My life is stable; it flows almost the same from one month to another; I grow up, argue with my sister, adapt, and find new ways to survive and be well. Then suddenly, everything changes.

I'm eight years old and have a newborn sister when Mom and Dad announce that we're moving, not just out of Syracuse, but leaving Sicily entirely.

WE ALL CHANGE, WE ALWAYS CHANGE

Everything is about to change, or rather; it already has.

From the moment I first opened my eyes, the changes I've faced have been too numerous to even imagine, much less count. Many of those changes saved my life, while others complicated it. All of them have written my story and shaped my responses.

My current mindset stems from how I've learned to react to various events and stimuli.

Our behavior, reactions, and thoughts are the result of countless stimuli and our interpretation of them.

We are who we are because we have done certain things, experienced certain chemical emotions, and acted accordingly. Our so-called character is formed by combining natural predisposition and the response to the environment around us. Chemistry plays a significant role in who we are.

When we feel fear, our amygdala stores that experience so that we can recall it whenever we encounter something similar.

When we feel safe, valued, and cared for, our brain releases oxytocin —the same hormone triggered during sex and before and after childbirth.

When we succeed in something we thought was impossible or very difficult, we produce dopamine, endorphins, and serotonin, which make us feel great, so much so that, in some cases, we become dependent on them, like runners, not only by running or repeating success but also by simply remembering it.

There is also biology in who we are.

We are all born equal. I'm not talking about people but living beings. When we come into the world, we are a single cell. A cell that then becomes two, trillions (in the case of humans), or a few thousand (for insects and plants). And for all living organisms, the first cells are all the same and then differentiate: some become part of the heart, others become nose hairs, and others work in high places, in what we call gray matter.

Change is constant: even when our cells have settled into specific functions and roles, they can continue to change throughout their lifespan. They can be trained and rewired, in other words, somehow reprogrammed. Even the brain cells, which we have discovered to be plastic in recent years, can change.

It would be much easier if we started learning how we function and why certain mechanisms lead us to behave in a specific way, starting from elementary school or even kindergarten. But it doesn't happen: school, from elementary to university, excludes the human being and its mechanisms from its programs.

What if, instead of being victims, we learned to shape our responses?

What if we learned to produce hormones on command, according to our needs?

And what if we learned to recognize and then remove the obstacles with which we have filled our paths in response to the environment?

Impossible? Time will tell.

LEARN TO UNLEARN

To free ourselves from our own constraints, we must first, inevitably, recognize them, know where they come from and why they exist, and then learn to defuse them.

What makes us feel good?
What makes us want to repeat a positive experience and simultaneously escape a negative one we've experienced before?
The emotions we feel (the good ones and the others).
Okay, clear emotions. But where do emotions come from, and what exactly are they?
According to the etymology of this word, emotions are related to movement (*emovere*, to move out, to bring out). If we add chemistry to history, we see that our emotions are offspring of certain neurotransmitters upon which our mood depends and which, in turn, lead us to respond in one way or another.

#SATISFACTION

We enter a store because we've seen a dress we like. Our memory is already activated in front of the shop window (whether made of glass or pixels doesn't really matter), and even before looking at the details of the item we're interested in, something in our brain has already been triggered.

We enter, and someone smiles at us, recognizes us, and calls us by name: we haven't touched or tried anything yet, but we already feel good. Serotonin is already circulating. The purchasing process goes smoothly, like oil. Everything works, there is no discomfort, and the product goes from the shop window to the cart and from there to us—more serotonin.

When we encounter no obstacles and bring home the desired object, the experience is a source of pleasure: hormones like dopamine and oxytocin are circulating, we feel good, and we experience satisfaction.

Let's say we're speaking in front of ten people or just one person who matters significantly to us. We're in front of an audience, and we're afraid.
We all are afraid. Even those who do it as a profession and have been doing it for a lifetime, as studies dating back to the 1970s demonstrate. According to David Wallechinsky, the author of "The Book of Lists," Among the 14 worst fears of human beings, the top spot is the fear of public speaking.

What's happening? Why are we sweating? Why does our tongue suddenly feel heavy, our throat tightens, and why do we lose our breath?
It's the fault of the amygdala—or rather, our fault for not understanding it and, therefore, not knowing how to control it.
The amygdala is a little almond-shaped thing (in ancient Greek, "amygdala" means almond) located in our prefrontal lobe. Its task is to analyze our experiences and label them as needed. If it perceives danger, it sends an emergency signal that stimulates the release of fight-or-flight hormones: adrenaline, dopamine, and norepinephrine.

So, when necessary, the amygdala sends signals to our motor centers and activates our cardiovascular system, muscles, and intestines. At the same time, it rushes to the archives - the mnemonic techniques - in search of helpful information to manage the situation. Suddenly, we remember that time when we made a fool of ourselves during an exam, or rather, we place a series of times when things went wrong, and the more we try not to think about it, the worse we feel. Trying not to think about the elephant just makes us think about elephants even more.
Once the amygdala wakes up, it does nothing but replays our worst

experiences, and it's so good at its job that even before we turn on our microphone, we feel the urge to run away (flight).

So are we doomed?

Not necessarily, especially if instead of racking our brains trying not to think about the elephant, we start petting it.

A suitable method, experts say, is to declare our fear to our audience: admitting to being nervous is a bit like hitting the snooze button; it's like telling our amygdala that we acknowledge its presence.

- Okay, thanks, I understand. I know we're nervous.

There's another step we can take, another approach we can implement to help us overcome discomfort and put our amygdala on standby: we can think about every time things went well for us. Just one instance is enough: recalling an event in which we succeeded, where everything went great, even better than we hoped, immediately makes us feel better.

Because our success makes us radiant and happy like Easter, and the associated emotions of response are imprinted in our memory forever and with such force that just recalling them, even without reliving them, makes us feel something similar again, even years later.

#FRUSTRATION

Returning to the shop story, we don't find what we were looking for (our size isn't available or the color we wanted), the procedure gets stuck, or if it's an online store, the pages don't load. And so, when something goes wrong, we feel frustration, sometimes sadness.

If we're in a brick-and-mortar store and encounter an employee who doesn't understand what we're looking for or isn't treating us the way we'd like, our frustration can escalate, even turning into anger. When faced with someone who should treat us with kid gloves but doesn't, we wonder why they don't change their job.

Why do you work in a store if you don't like dealing with people? We ask ourselves.

Yet there's another question we should ask, especially every time we face another person, whether in person or remotely: what have we done to establish a connection with this human being who ignores us? Maybe they're busy, and perhaps they're trying to solve a big problem... What's this person's name? And who is this person?

Before asking for attention, have we given any?

I don't mean to say that it all depends on us. Certainly, we can't do anything if the other person doesn't listen to us, responds poorly, or doesn't feel like paying attention, just as we can't do anything if our size is out of stock. However, it's different when something in the experience we're going through makes us feel inadequate and causes us discomfort if we're laughed at when asking for our size (regardless of what size it is).

Or if we're looked at as not up to the situation. That's when it becomes bullying.

Sticking to the example of the store, a few months ago, I read a book that made me discover the existence of so-called fatphobia and led me to a series of reflections.

The book in question was written by Chiara Meloni and Mara Mibelli, published in 2021 by Mondadori with the authors' Instagram profile title: "Belle di faccia. Tecniche per ribellarsi a un mondo grassofobico" ("Pretty Faces: Techniques to Rebel Against a Fatphobic World").

"We're not curvy; we're fat," write Chiara and Mara. "We're not soft; keep that adjective for sofas and mattresses. We're fat. In a society where fat bodies are perpetually pathologized and likened to an epidemic (we swear we haven't infected anyone), using the word 'fat' without a negative connotation has been a liberation, a revolution. Many people correct us when we call ourselves fat, and the most common response is usually, 'No, but you're beautiful as you are.' When have we ever said otherwise?"

The two authors immediately warn me that reading their book won't be relaxing, *"but then again, being fat in a fatphobic world isn't either. The humiliations, the insults, the microaggressions, and our excessive passion for listing these uglinesses have led us to become the people we are. Now we launch 'fuck you' like ninja stars. Unstoppable like Chuck Norris, ruthless like Ivan Drago, imperturbable like Nicholas Cage's face (yes, we've watched many action movies with our parents). Because this is the only true detox we have to do, the only toxin we have to eliminate: kicking fatphobia in the ass, both outside and within us."*

Our society is evidently fatphobic, just as, going back to the textbooks of middle school and art history books, they were highly thin-phobic. Today, in a nutshell, we attribute status to thin people that, until half a century ago, belonged to the elites, the rich, in other words, the coolest.

Since the late 1960s, with the first major feminist movements, the ideal female body has become thin. This is also a collective response, but it is a response: to make it clear that our bodies are our own and not objects of the patriarchy; they don't have to be shapely; in fact, the thinner they are, the better. Twiggy and later Kate Moss established the canon upon which fashion has been modeled, aside from all the hot air.

A woman is expected to be thin, very thin, and it's never thin enough, especially when you consider that store displays, both in-person and online, still feature mannequins that are over seven feet tall, with limbs thinner than Barbie dolls. In some stores, I'm told that the sizes are limited to three, with the largest being a size forty.

These stereotypes, clichés, and images are imprinted on us, shaping our perception of the world and its values. And in this universe we find ourselves living in, the central stereotypes are still linked to the survival of the species. And if we think about it and listen to anthropologists, not much has changed in the last two hundred thousand years: we are still attracted to those who are stronger and more resilient. In other words, to those who can hunt alongside us, help protect our cave, and reproduce.

If someone is in shape (the precise-identical shape we see on Instagram), it means they can take care of themselves, and if they can do that, it's because they have time, which means they're not just wealthy but even successful.

At the same time, *driving a premium car* is the new equivalent of *wielding a big club*. If someone drives an expensive car, it means they can afford it, which means they know how to "hunt."

But we can make the same argument for public success, followers, recognition, and roles. The CEO is the new clan leader, and the board of directors is the new council of elders.

If we genuinely want to learn to unlearn, we must first realize that clothing has changed, but the rest hasn't changed so much. We are still victims of an ancestral legacy that may not always be useful and not for everyone.

FEAR

THE ANTHROPOLOGY OF FEAR OF CONTACT

Since the dawn of time, humans have had a great fear of being touched by the unknown. Contact with the unfamiliar scares us, causing us to run away, build barriers and safeguards around ourselves, arm ourselves, and get organized.

"The fear of being touched dictates all the distances people have created around themselves. We shut ourselves in houses where no one can enter; only we feel relatively safe there. The aversion to being touched does not leave us even when we are among people. The way we move on the street, among many people, in a restaurant, on a train, on a bus, is dictated by that fear. Even when we are very close to others, able to observe and study them well, we avoid touching them as much as possible." (Elias Canetti)

Elias Canetti is the author of 'Crowds and Power,' a groundbreaking work that explores why humans are so repelled by random and unfamiliar contact while also being drawn to groups and crowds.

We're so scared of being touched or coming into contact with strangers that we react instantly. Among people, if someone accidentally touches us, we immediately pull away or jump back as if shocked, and others do the same when we touch them.

Here it is, the fear of raising a finger and making contact with someone we don't know.

We need to talk to Maria because we have realized that Maria is the person who can help us in the endeavor we are undertaking. It's her;

it's definitely her. We're sure because we've taken the time to find out who she is, how she communicates, and what she does. But even though we know she can help us, and even though we have decided to contact her, and maybe we have even planned it in our daily journals and lists, we continue to hesitate. Instead of raising a finger and opening contact with Maria, we procrastinate.

What are we afraid of?
Of rejection. Of a no. And even of silence alone.

We're afraid of being ignored or not even getting a response. We fear that the Maria in question is too high up to deign to respond to us, that she is too important to care about us, that she is too far away.

We all know the theory of six degrees of separation, right? The one that says that every human being can come into contact with anyone in the world through no more than five intermediaries.

First formulated in 1929 by Frigyes Karinthy, the original theory stated that every person could be connected to anyone else through five steps. In the late 1960s, American psychologist Stanley Milgram conducted a social experiment to test his 'small world' theory: he selected a random group of people in the Midwest. He asked them to send a package to a stranger in Massachusetts, knowing only the recipient's name but not the address. It took the boxes between five and seven steps to reach their destination, and his theory was published in Psychology Today, giving rise to the expression "six degrees of separation." Then the internet arrived, and about twenty years later, in 2011, the computer science department of the University of Milan, along with two Facebook researchers, demonstrated that the degrees of separation could be as low as four.

Between us and Maria,[10] whomever she is and whatever role she occupies, there is very little distance: according to the theory, even if Maria were an empress or a pope, in less than five steps, we could contact her.

So why don't we try?

Again, it's because we are terrified of rejection; if we are, it's because

---

[10] From here on, I may as well stop using italics to refer to Maria, right?

we are filled with fears, many of which are self-produced and carefully stored in our heads by the amygdala.

If we're so anxious about a NO that wouldn't actually change our lives, then we've spent our whole lives building defenses that, more often than not, turn into walls, which were meant to protect us but have become prisons instead.

We shield ourselves with clothing, masks, roles, labels, and defense mechanisms, all rooted in our deep-seated and age-old fear of being touched by the unknown.

#STORY OF A REQUEST

I'm a part of many networks and well-known for mentoring young leaders globally; I get lots of requests for advice, and I never hesitate to share my knowledge. Sharing my experience is a great and productive way to give back to the community.

Some time ago, a girl contacted me from one of these networks. She was finishing her master's degree at Lehigh University, and since the algorithm had indicated possible compatibility, she reached out to me, and we got in touch.

During our first meeting, she told me that she had tried reaching out to nine other people worldwide, all suggested by the algorithm, but I was the only one who responded. This really drives me nuts. What's so hard about just replying? And then, when I think about the times I sought contact in an unfamiliar environment, the only silence I received came not from the top individuals in the field but from ordinary, very ordinary people. It demonstrates how the best behaviors always come from the best people.

The mediocre person has no time for others. They feel too high and mighty to pay attention to the rest of the world, feeling accomplished and even unattainable. In my experience, it has been easier for me to connect with significant individuals than with so-called "wannabes."

It's crucial to teach younger generations that dedicating yourself to others is the best way to serve the community. It is our investment in the well-being of the country. "The way to grow your power is to give it away," Carla Harris[11], said in her memorable TED Talk.

This young American girl, with Asian origins and the first in her family to graduate, was seeking guidance and mentorship. She was looking for someone to fill that role.

Despite getting eight rejections, she kept asking—either she wasn't scared, or she managed her fear well. Either way, she kept at it until she got a yes.

Fear of asking is usually the reason why successful connections don't happen. Asking for someone's time for a video call, asking for participation in an event we are organizing, asking to join a free webinar, asking for advice on a job opportunity abroad, or even from someone present in our lives as a mentor and asking for help.

It happens to everyone every day. And if it happens, it's because we receive conflicting messages from a young age. The female world grows with the idea of needing a male whom they must care for as long as they have the strength. Still, at the same time, there is a desperate need to do without, to break free from a certain patriarchal stereotype, to emerge and assert themselves as individuals and no longer as compliant companions. Moreover, for me and countless other women, we were taught not to ask for help to figure things out on our own, especially regarding household matters. These teachings have become so ingrained that many people are averse to delegating. Despite the numerous tasks we need to take care of in our homes, we struggle to ask for help even from the rest of our families. There are laundry loads to be done, and even if our schedules are on the verge of collapse, we take care of it ourselves. But why?

Why is it that when I ask for help, I already know I'll hear "yes," but later or tomorrow? And why, right after that, will they ask me about the temperature, which program, and whether pink and white can go together?

Of course, they can, then we'll have a whole series of pink underwear and shirts, but pink is a nice color, isn't it?

So why is it easier for me to do it than explain it?

---

[11] "The way to grow your power is to give it to others" - Sponsors are the people who use their power to get you noticed by the higher-ups. Here's how to find yours.
Watch the full TED Talk here: http://t.ted.com/w8DQUoZ

Also, let's be honest, the whole idea of 'help' is flawed: if we're living under the same roof or in the same 'tribe,' to use Canetti's term, then we should all be taking care of each other anyway. But no, if you're born a woman and want to work and enjoy this incredible career privilege, this enlightened concession, you can't afford to neglect the rest. Not at all.

If you really want to work, make sure everything else is in order.

Whose fault is it? They say the system and patriarchy, but I believe - and I'm not alone - that it's primarily our fault that we still raise our (male) children by caring for them like princes while teaching the females to care for the males and the elderly.

The male universe, on the other hand, despite still living in privilege, isn't much better off. Boys are told that they shouldn't cry, show emotions, or appear fragile; they're supposed to be strong and successful. As for me, I'm deeply convinced that my travels between America, India, Israel, Northern Europe, and the Balkans, ever since my son was a year and a half old, have given him an edge: he may have missed me at times, but when I look at him today, in the midst of adolescence, I see a boy capable of taking care of himself and maneuvering through life, while his peers (and not just them) depend on their mothers for everything, including laundry and cooking. He knows how to do everything and seems to do it willingly.

Going back to the fear of raising a finger and the previous fear of rejection, instead of fantasizing, let's see what could actually happen if they say no.

Feeling rejected reminds us of failure.
They said no, so I'm not good enough.
They said no, so my idea wasn't innovative enough.
They said no, I must be really ordinary.

Yet, deep down, the negative interpretation of the sequence is nothing more than the concatenation of incompatible events, revealing all our prejudices and insecurities.

To overcome the barrier of fear to ask, we must work on our self-esteem. It's like when we want a more upright posture, with a straight back, so we tighten our buttocks. In the case of self-esteem, we must work on our communication. Communication and how we use words and body language are the straight back.

Communicating confidently and clearly gives us a straight back as if we were tightening our buttocks.

We cannot control what others say or how they behave, but we can decide what to say and how.

How we say what we're about to say. The tone and the body language we use. And the type of communication I'm talking about has nothing to do with NLP, neuro-linguistic programming: it's not manipulation, and it's not about aligning our energy with the universe. It's not about "The law of attraction teaches us to get what we want by using the power of our mind and the positivity of our thoughts."

Choosing words and deciding how to use them is the key to writing the story we want to read: ours, first and foremost, as it has been proven that the words we use to describe a specific event can alter our mood.

To experiment, I'll tell you one of my worst experiences. Here's what happened.

I was working as a lawyer in a clinic when I realized something was off. One of the executives behaved detrimental to the company's profit, disregarding the patients' health. I'm obsessed with justice, and for me, it's inconceivable for someone to take advantage of their client's good faith. So, I went straight to the person in question and blurted out everything. I confronted him, and in doing so, I unleashed the anger I felt to the point that I soon found myself without a job: fired on the spot.

What did I achieve? The guy stayed in his position and continued to do very wrong things while I was thrown out and found myself at home, struggling to make ends meet with a young child and a thousand responsibilities. I blamed myself and felt terrible every time I thought about it.

From then on, for years, I (and even to myself) retold this story using words that highlighted my emotional state at that time—anger, remorse, you name it. Whenever I talked about it, I felt the same negative emotions, as if I were still in front of that person or had just been fired.

Then I changed my approach and mindset, or - as someone would say - I modified the "storytelling" of the whole thing (!) and started talking about it with lightness as if I were always facing a child.

I was the lawyer in a large clinic where someone was doing a poor job and committing real injustices, and I went to tell him to his face without even thinking about what I wanted to achieve. While talking to this person, I let the anger for all the injustices in the world pour onto him as if he were a universal scapegoat. He ensured I stayed home so I finally had time to figure out what I wanted. And thank goodness or I wouldn't be here today, and I wouldn't be so happy.

Although my intentions back then were undoubtedly good (justice! doing things correctly, patients' health, etc.), my way of throwing it all in the culprit's face wasn't helpful. On the contrary.
From that experience, I didn't just bring home a friendly termination letter but also a couple of valuable lessons.

1. The first is the awareness that honesty is a good thing, but it needs to be balanced, or it risks turning into judgment and becoming a boomerang.

2. The second is the awareness that our words are not just words but triggers.

Triggers kick things off, engage us, and activate the underlying mechanisms that run our lives.
Recognizing them allows us to learn how to use them and, above all, to stop being their victims.

All you need is... NET

Thanks to internet technology, "everyone is connected."

We hear this all the time, particularly when we witnessed the rapid spread of the Coronavirus, which crossed international borders in just a matter of days. Since we have already talked about the word "network," let's now delve into the network and ask ourselves what makes all networks essential for human beings.

To explore this, let's revisit Elias Canetti's ideas from 'Crowds and Power.' He argues that we stop fearing others only when we're in a crowd. He attributes the formation of crowds to four different types of 'muta' (akin to 'molt,' or changes sparked by various causes in small groups): hunting, war, lament, and growth.

Let's compare the history of our origins to what we still experience today around us every day. We discover that the mechanisms that move us (muta comes from the medieval Latin "movita," meaning movement) are still the same.

Before it's defined by business codes, tax identification numbers, and revenue, a company is essentially a community of people. Within this community, you can find different forms of 'muta': hunting muta, war muta, and aggregation muta. And quite frequently, there's also lament muta. After all, you don't need a death to hear complaints or lamentations echoing in the hallways of organizations all over the world, right?

But a family is also a muta.

Just as a community is a crowd, so is a network of people united by ideals, interests, and affinities: on social media, hashtags bring us together, and behind them are algorithms; but before social media, it was books, readings, schools of thought, or clubs of any kind.

We unite to join a community that shares our beliefs, and each time we're accepted by that community, we grow stronger. Conversely, if it doesn't happen, and for some reason, we remain outside, we experience exclusion as a failure.

Failure is frightening because we've all heard countless stories about it. In modern folklore, failures have all but replaced the traditional figures of village fools, outsiders, renegades, and exiles. In a century where success is everything, failure is inevitably its nemesis, the ultimate enemy: if you have everything you need to succeed, and it's just a click away, wherever you are, it also means that you can't fail, and if you do, you're worthless.

It's as if the narrative of success and its exaggeration has divided humanity into two factions: on one side, those who have made it, and on the other, those who haven't even tried.

Before he became President, Lincoln lost ten elections.

Walt Disney was fired for "lack of imagination and no good ideas," and his first animation studio went bankrupt.

J.K. Rowling's first Harry Potter novel was rejected twelve times; Anne Frank's diary received fifteen rejections; Stephen King's collected thirty; Lewis, the author of The Chronicles of Narnia, piled over eight hundred rejections. Hemingway was told that his first novel, Fiesta, was both tedious and offensive. Nabokov experienced something similar with his novel Lolita.[12]

Before founding Alibaba, Jack Ma failed twice.

His high school basketball team rejected Michael Jordan.

Einstein was slow at school and received one low grade after another.

Oprah Winfrey was immediately fired and told she wasn't fit for television.

It doesn't matter that the history of "winners" and their hall of fame is filled with consecutive failures: if we know about their attempts and failures, it's because they didn't give up even in the face of disappointment, and eventually, they succeeded.

Having expectations doesn't mean they have to happen by force.

Expectations reflect the hopes we hold, but our lives are actually

---

[12] [https://www.ilpost.it/2014/06/11/lettere-rifiuto-grandi-scrittori/]

shaped by actions, reactions, and outcomes.

No expectations, not "let's hope it happens," but repeated actions supported by a purpose that must be precise, organized, consistent, and, as Albert Hirschman says about the principle of the "hidden hand" in project management, even unrealistically optimistic.

"Social planners in underdeveloped countries must be unrealistically optimistic; no project would be undertaken if they were realistic. They underestimate threats and their own responses to failure. They also overestimate the chances of success. They overlook possible and unsuspected threats to profitability and even the project's existence. The link to the planning fallacy begins here. But through human creativity, they find unexpected solutions. Hiding the hand benevolently conceals the difficulties, and the result is just as predicted or even better than they thought. This is assured by providential ignorance."

Having an 'unrealistically optimistic' goal helps us anchor new options that are unthinkable, unexpected, and unanticipated.

We must look beyond failure, not ignore it, but consider it a way to find new paths.

As Nietzsche once said, "What doesn't kill me makes me stronger."

Today, the time is ripe to tell the story of failure as a resource to learn and be inspired.

#THINK OUT OF THE BOX

A while back, 'thinking outside the box' was all the rage, and the phrase, which originated in America, has been so impactful that we still hear it today. "Thinking outside the box" is, in itself, impossible, considering how our brain works: first, because to think outside the box, we would need to know exactly which box we are talking about; second, because our knowledge about the brain is still significantly lacking. Thirdly, as Wittgenstein pointed out, we already include the answer within the question as soon as we ask it, thereby trying to systematize something.

If the question itself, as it is posed, conditions its solution, then the solution lies within the framework, not outside. Instead of trying to escape from a framework we often don't even see, we can flip it over and turn it upside down. Thinking outside the box isn't the solution: what really matters is asking ourselves the right questions in the right way, knowing what we want, where we aim to go, and why, overcoming obstacles, moving forward, learning from failures, and making adjustments to improve

Rewinding, erasing, and starting again.

There are no excuses. It's just us, our path, and only one option: to succeed.

What stops us?

In reality, no one holds us back, yet something does. Something still holds us back. All the factors I've just mentioned (the success of others, the failures of those who've succeeded before, the fear of inadequacy) make everything seem overwhelming, too complicated, and too far out of reach, to the point that fear of failure stops us from even starting three out of four times.

#THE PERFECTION TRAP

> «*It is a pity to do nothing on the pretext that we cannot do everything.* »
> ***Winston Churchill***

We grow up inundated with narratives that glorify absolute excellence and perfection: if something is not excellent, it doesn't deserve to exist, and above all, it doesn't deserve to be shared, shown to the world, and made public.

The pursuit of perfection follows us from one decade to another, starting with grades in school. While they mark the divide between deserving and undeserving students, they encourage the former and demotivate the latter. We become adults fixated on numbers: the GPAs of our degrees, the horsepower of our cars, the square footage of our homes, the digits in our salaries, and the follower counts on our social media profiles that we obsessively check—until we eventually stop caring because the platform becomes outdated or loses its youthful appeal.

And yet, "*perfect*" comes from something achieved or complete, not from excellent, not from superb, or flawless, because as the theory of relativity (widely demonstrated) teaches us, there is nothing genuinely perfect, and certainly not for everyone. And so, in pursuing perfection, fearing that we won't achieve it, we don't even begin.

We try to connect with someone, start typing a message, and then pause after the third line. The cursor blinks on the screen. We reread what we just wrote, go back to looking at the profile of the person in question, and delete everything. We try other words, more elegant, more formal. We reread it, find it insincere, or spot something that seems off, so we hit DELETE: our message isn't up to snuff and doesn't merit being sent.

This perfection trap hinders us daily in much of what we do; what's worse, while making us feel inadequate, it also prevents us from improving or, in some cases, even taking action.

The fear of failure, rejection, and the performance anxiety associated with excellence make us end up like a fly caught in a spider's web. The difference is that here, we are both the fly and the spider, and even the spider's web, and until we realize this, there is no way out.

Since our brain flees from the unknown, and our system, as living beings, operates on repeated patterns, the only way to make things work (to establish a connection, build a series of relationships, as well as learn to pilot a Boeing or stop making movies in our heads) is to learn to control our patterns.

Alright, so how long does this take?

To start, it takes twenty-one days.
> «*Continuous improvement is better than delayed perfection.* »
> Mark Twain

#21 DAYS

"In 1960, Dr. Maxwell, who had just turned 61 and had performed thousands of plastic surgeries, published a book in which he revealed that, based on his experience, it takes people 21 days to adjust to their new appearance. In practical terms: 21 days to change.

This is the origin of the theory of the 21-day rule, which suggests that it only takes three weeks to incorporate a change into our lives (such as a new habit) and make it stable.

Franco Berrino, meditation expert Daniel Lumera, and coach David Mariani also explore the same 21-day timeframe in their 2020 book, "Ventuno giorni per rinascere" (Twenty-One Days to Be Reborn):

"Scientific studies and ancient Eastern and South American traditions suggest that twenty-one days represent the minimum time for a habit to become part of our lives. We have proposed to achieve three main objectives within this timeframe: purify, rejuvenate, and prolong life."[13]

Returning to Dr. Maxwell, his book, "Psycho-Cybernetics," laid the foundation for numerous personal development movements, including Neuro-Linguistic Programming (NLP). He explains that each of us has our inner image (self-image) that can be "improved" through various methodologies. According to Dr. Maxwell, the soul, and psyche often need reshaping more than the skin and body.

Although the title may sound like something out of science fiction, it's worth noting that cybernetics is the scientific study of self-regulation and communication in both natural and artificial systems. Combining the two words (psychology plus cybernetics) refers to how we can work on our self-image to achieve any goal.

This thesis, which is embraced by modern psychology, aims to show why the success of some individuals and the failure of others are linked to their self-image.

---

[13] [https://www.huffingtonpost.it/2018/03/28/bastano-21-giorni-per-rinascere-iniziate-con-queste-buone-abitudini_a_23396751/]

*

I was in the car with my secretary, Anna, on our way to the courthouse. While we were discussing what needed to be done before the hearings, I asked her at one point how she saw me.

Anna turned abruptly. "Excuse me? What do you mean?"

"I mean, I want a definition, exactly," I replied.

I've been involved in quality management for a long time, specifically in total quality management. I was still mentoring some people while gaining experience as a leadership and communication trainer. Additionally, I opened a language immersion preschool. So, was I a quality consultant? Was I a socially active entrepreneur? Was I a leadership developer?
In Italy every worker needs to be labeled with a title or a definition. I was looking for my definition.
"What a strange question..." Anna said.

"Yes, but who am I to you?" I asked.

"To me, you are Attorney Irene Magistro."

It was the first time I'd heard someone say that, and it sounded strange to me. It didn't feel entirely mine; no one in my family (all pharmacists) had passed the torch to me, and no one had instructed me about the value of the legal profession. Yet here was Anna, seeing me with the title I had earned with so much effort, achieved seven years late.

About a decade later, after practicing law for so long, I had to give it up because it was incompatible with my role as a company administrator. This shook me up for a while; a friend, a former high school classmate, and a lawyer started calling me "Doctor" as soon as I removed myself from the bar due to this incompatibility, and I took offense. For years, I associated the word "lawyer" with the role, the robe, the attire, and its weight in society, and suddenly, I felt exposed.

There is a saying I've only heard in English, and it goes like this:
"FAKE IT UNTIL YOU MAKE IT."
But there is an updated version of this phrase, and it is
"FAKE IT UNTIL YOU BECOME IT."
And indeed, I had pretended to be a lawyer until I became one.

I imagine that during the construction of our professional identity, we all wear a costume and go to the "theater" every day until we become what we pretend to be.

In the end, we are simply OURSELVES.

Even our origins are important.

I had colleagues who had grown up with "bread and law," as I like to say, meaning they had acquired the language from birth, from one or both parents who were lawyers. I had eaten "bread and medicine" because my parents were pharmacists.

How we see ourselves influences how we feel and, and therefore,
what we can achieve.

Whether we have a title or not, what we are and will always be is human beings.

If we want to connect with the world around us, we must remember that we are all equal. Humanity is the trait that unites us all, regardless of color, religion, political opinion, profession, language, or social background. We are human. In every encounter and interaction, we should always remember that this is what we are: human beings, living beings, imperfect in every way except for being human.

When our perception of ourselves is negative, perhaps trapped in the past, anchored to one or more unhappy episodes we have experienced, it becomes difficult for us to break free. And when we chase the myth of absolute excellence and pursue perfection, we are so afraid of failure that we risk not even starting.

There are hundreds of good books and podcasts that can help us escape our own traps. Most of these resources focus on the same principles, the first of which is to stop engaging in destructive behaviors or, in other words, to break bad habits.

"The most successful people in the world constantly recognize the things that don't work for them and stop doing them. These people have perseverance; they don't give up in the usual sense of the term. They act responsibly by putting effort into their work, relationships, careers, or teams and doing their best—but then, after doing so, they also have enough discernment to understand when they need to move on. Certain jobs, relationships, or teams either bore them, make them unhappy, or simply don't offer the excitement that other options might. So, decisively and boldly, high performers cut ties and put their efforts into something else."

Advanced Habits for Career Success, The Brendon Show (The Charged Life) podcast, Brendon Burchard.

In Atomic Habits, James Clear, one of the world's leading experts on habit formation, argues that to create good habits, break bad ones, and improve by 1% every day, we must first stop believing that the problem is ourselves.

"If you're having trouble changing your habits, the problem is not you. The problem is your system."

WE ALWAYS COPY. WE COPY EVERYONE

- But are we sure it's yours?
- Of course.
- Maybe, but I've already heard this somewhere.
- No, it's mine.
- But I feel like I've already read it.
- I'm telling you it's mine.

Everything I'm writing, I've thought of and written myself, so this book is all mine. It's authentic. It's original. But everything I believe, have thought and will think doesn't come out of nowhere. And if it doesn't come out of nowhere, it must come from somewhere, which leads me to doubt that this book is truly mine.

I used the word "book" because we all tend to get attached to things we consider ourselves and defend the originality of our creations. But if we substitute the book for a movie, a photograph, an algorithm's code, a business model, or PowerPoint slides, the outcome remains the same.

We feel such ownership over our thoughts that when we discuss them as intellectual works, we label them as intellectual property.

"Property" - a real right placed on a thing, which gives its holder the immediate and absolute power to do whatever they want with the thing itself: to keep it with them and enjoy it, to dispose of it, and even to destroy it if they wish.

Indeed, there's an entire branch of law dedicated to intellectual property, aimed at protecting authorship rights through various clauses and rulings.

But no thought, ever, is truly and solely ours.

"There is no thought without precedents," writes Siri Hustvedt in her essay "The Illusions of Certainty."

> *"In a sense, all ideas are acquired; they come from somewhere."*

Everything we think, produce, and then spread has at least two parents. Parent one is the context in which we live, with all the instincts we are made of, the patterns we operate with, and the stimuli we have received over time. Parent two is our response to the events we have experienced.

Everything we make manifest leaves a trace that nourishes the two aforementioned parents and thus influences people's thoughts and spreads.

"The languages of our ideas are contagious. Words travel from one person to another, and we can all be influenced by ideas that can last a lifetime. Humans are the only animals who kill for ideas, so it's wise to take them seriously and ask what they are and where they come from."

In the 1980s, when Jane Fonda showed up on TV doing aerobics, everyone rushed out to buy leg warmers. Suddenly aerobics became popular: we like it and need it. In the same decade, along with short pants and high waists (as I'm writing again among ourselves), the word "cioè" (which means "that is" in Italian) also emerged and immediately became popular. In the 1990s, *"piuttosto che"* (which means "rather than" in Italian) gains ground as an alternative to "oppure" (which means "or" in Italian).

In the 2000s, *resilience* jumped out of its context and invaded all the others. Until a second before, it was quietly sitting on the technical shelf, indicating the capacity of a material to absorb energy when subjected to elastic deformation, and the next second it had already become a buzzword: a magical word that is everywhere like parsley in Agee restaurants.

In 2008, *hipsters* appeared.

In 2018, *boomers*[14] were.

Then ableism (entered in the new words of the Accademia della Crusca[15] in June 2021[16]). Catcalling, machismo, body norms, and the adjectives toxic and challenging

From year to year, certain ideas—like fashion and thoughts—come into vogue, while others suddenly become taboo, almost as if they've been blacklisted overnight.
The word with the letter "n."
"But Mom, why do we say 'people of color'?" my son asks me one day. I look at him, and as I think about how to answer him, he anticipates me by touching my face: "Doesn't it seem strange to you? he says, we're all colorful. We are pink."

This conversation dates back to 2010. At the time, my son is four years old and sees what many adults fail to see.

Even certain specific endings become a delicate subject, and we see bizarre signs, asterisks, and the schwa, replacing gender declensions.

We can't help but wonder: What makes a word go viral? What turns an idea into a trend? What turns a trend into a need? What makes the thought of an individual become the thought of a mass? What makes something mainstream? Why - suddenly - do we all, I mean all, talk about resilience? About mindset, leadership, motivation, discomfort,

---

[14] The term baby boom refers to a noticeable increase in the birth rate. The post-World War II population increase was described as a "boom" by various newspaper reporters, including Sylvia F. Porter in a column in the May 4, 1951, edition of the New York Post, based on the increase of 2,357,000 in the population of the U.S. from 1940 to 1950. The first recorded use of "baby boomer" is in a January 1963 Daily Press article by Leslie J. Nason describing a massive surge of college enrollments approaching as the oldest boomers were coming of age.[24][25] The Oxford English Dictionary dates the modern meaning of the term to a January 23, 1970, article in The Washington Post.

[15] https://en.wikipedia.org/wiki/Accademia_della_Crusca

[16] 2006 «Oliver concludes by hoping that "after reading this book, ableism can be placed at the bottom of the list because disability deserves to be the subject of sociological analysis and demystification exactly like the other 'isms'" (Oliver, 1990 , p.131)" (Enrico Valtellina, "Nothing about us without us". From activism to academia and back: English "disability studies", in "Studi cultural, quarterly review", 1/2006, pp. 159 -180). [https://accademiadellacrusca.it/it/parole-nuove/abilismo/18496]

anxiety?

Why do we say "like" this and that?

"Like, this article will be like read by, like, twenty-one people who will like, negatively comment on the use of the word 'like.'"[17]

Jung talks about the collective unconscious, a sort of universal psychic box containing a series of symbols/references that he calls archetypes common to all human beings in the history of the world.

Daniel Kahneman, Nobel laureate in economics in 2002, argues that our brain uses a series of shortcuts to simplify things (known as heuristics). In practice, we use patterns to do anything and make any decision with minimal effort. This leads us to a series of systematic errors we tend to make by relying on constructs outside of critical judgment, known as cognitive biases. According to Kahneman, biases are "predictable prejudices that occur in particular circumstances," as if we are not the ones choosing, but someone else.

And perhaps that's exactly it: when we think about it, we are not the ones who genuinely choose, not really, and not entirely. Whenever we feel scared, the amygdala reminds us of something unpleasant that happened to us and projected a film that scares us even more.

Okay, but the amygdala is ours, right?

Of course, it's ours; if it's in our brain, whose could it be? It's just that, like our thoughts, ideas, and intellectual works, the amygdala also has two parents: context and responses.

We may want to connect with a specific person, but even before reaching out to them—long before the possibility of rejection—we already feel growing discomfort, sensations akin to failure, and the urge to flee. We give up.

We start a conversation with a person we don't know. This person is talking to us, but we don't really hear them. Our ears receive the sounds they emit, and our brain decrypts them, giving them meaning. While the eardrum vibrates, our memory travels, make associations,

---

[17] [https://oltreuomo.com/le-12-parole-piu-volgarmente-abusate-dellitaliano-parlato/]

compares, and schematizes. Essentially, it reduces the person in front of us to a box and its corresponding label. We see their role - the lawyer, the director - and their badges - the degree, the master's; we see their followers. We see their status, and we see their posts, and sometimes even their homes. We don't REALLY know the person: we see the system in which our brain has enveloped them.

The problem is that establishing a connection is impossible if we don't hear this person, and we can't really see them.

Unless we step out of our comfort zone, which is our metaphorical couch, we can't really put ourselves in someone else's shoes. And if we can't get into those shoes, we can't honestly know who the other person is and what they need.

If we don't break free from our usual patterns and rid ourselves of our preconceptions, we can't truly open up to others or establish a genuine, mutually beneficial empathy. Unless...

WE ALWAYS LIE. WE ALL LIE

While researching for this chapter—before it even became a chapter—I asked myself, What is the mind? As I tried to focus my thoughts, a series of images, expressions, a couple of adverbs, and a verb came to mind. 'Fake it until you make it.' 'Good blood doesn't lie.' The two adverbs automatically and consciously; the verb 'to lie.'

But what exactly is the mind? In search of an answer, like I always do when I'm unsure or don't know something, I started researching, discovering that the Latin root of the word 'mind' (mens, from which comes 'mens sana in corpore sano') comes from the Indo-European 'man, men, or mein,' which made me think of 'man.' From there, I looked for a medical definition, then one more related to psychology, and philosophy, sliding between poetry and quotes offered by Google Images.

The issue is I didn't find just one answer; I found hundreds.

A few days later, when I started 'The Illusions of Certainty,' I read that Siri Hustvedt had asked herself the same question before writing her essay. While preparing to write her essay, Siri asked different people what the mind meant to them. 'I was genuinely curious to know what they thought. [...] Several seemed puzzled by my question.'

At that moment, I burst out laughing. Additionally, while researching the chapter on cognitive biases, I realized I was experiencing one firsthand:

Siri Hustvedt is an exceptional writer who also won the Princess of Asturias Award for Literature (in 2019), an accolade also received by J.K. Rowling, Woody Allen, Umberto Eco, Simone Weil, Margaret Atwood, among others.

If Siri (significant to me and recognized by the world) asked herself the same question and asked others, then I am on the right track.

I also wondered if it made sense to bring up the question in my work, especially since I was reading a book about the same topic by an author much more acclaimed than myself.

So I made a decision: I chose not only to discuss the mind but also to share my journey exploring why we all lie so frequently. From the mind, I then moved on to the mechanisms that lead us to lie and why it happens so often.

If we lie from a young age, as psychology says, it's because as soon as we start communicating, our brains understand that certain behaviors are acceptable (and bring us rewards) and others work against us.

We lie to avoid punishment.

Did you eat the candies?

No.

We lie to avoid a bad grade:

I did my homework, but the cat ate them.

We lie to please the boy who tells us he likes a certain album from a certain band that we wouldn't even know how to name.

Me too, you have no idea.

We lie about our weight (an obsession for many), height, and age (exaggerating when we're young and downplaying it as we get older). We lie with words and through filters: to receive approval, sell more, and convince someone.

When someone we care about asks for our opinion, and something feels off to us, we're often more inclined to lie rather than speak up honestly.

We rationalize it by telling ourselves it's for a good cause and immediately think of what are often called 'white lies.

Our friend asks how a particular dress looks on her: it looks terrible, but we don't want to offend her, so we say it looks fine.

We lie not just with our words but also through omission, leaving out the information we believe could hurt someone else—and by extension, us.

If we anticipate a conflict, our brain reacts with flight. Even if it's called the fight or flight response, the truth is that our brain only fights when it can't escape, so it tends to run away from any potential conflict.

Intellectual Stripper

We lie to avoid conflicts.
Are you angry?
No.
Sure?
Sure.
We lie when giving feedback.

After leading various teams in high-tech companies like AdSense, YouTube, Google, Apple University, Dropbox, Twitter, and others, Kim Scott realized that the most important thing for creating a good work environment was (and is) feedback, literally the 'nourishment of return.'

In her book 'Radical Candor: Be a Kickass Boss Without Losing Your Humanity,' Kim Scott introduces a framework for how we typically give feedback.

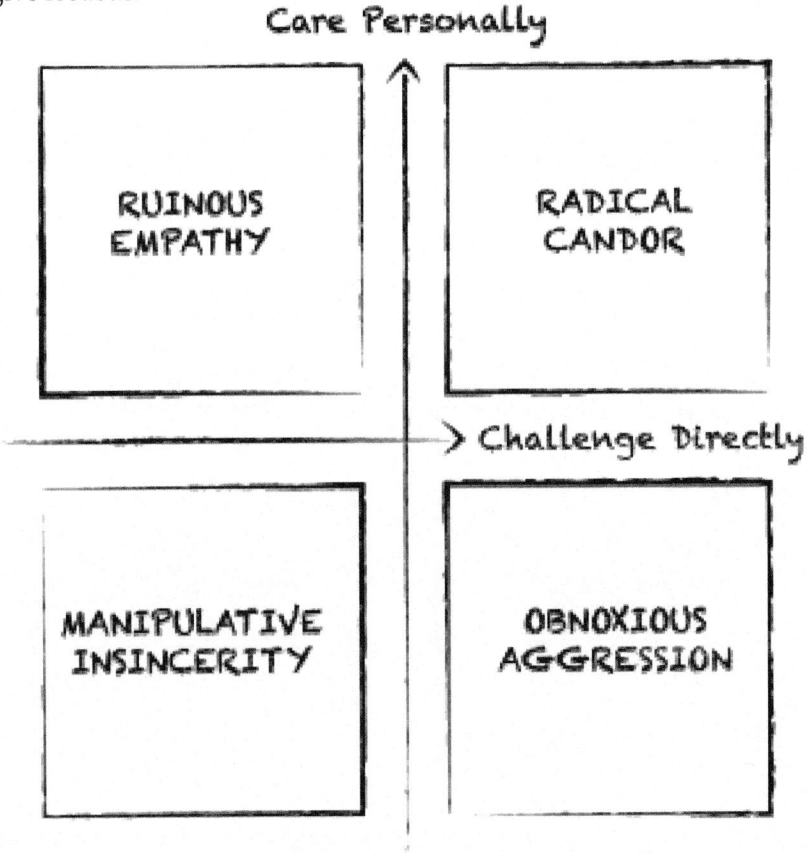

https://kimmalonescott.com/

When asked for feedback, we all know we should be honest. Some of us also know that we should provide it based on facts, careful not to shift the focus from the event to the person involved.

The problem is that "radical honesty," Kim's radical candor, is as rare as relevant.

Guidance is the single most important aspect of managing people.

In the matrix, the Y-axis represents the willingness to care for others, and the X-axis represents the willingness to 'challenge directly.' According to Kim, great leaders occupy the upper right quadrant, the radical candor, because they demonstrate concern for the well-being of their employees while also feeling a moral duty to challenge them.

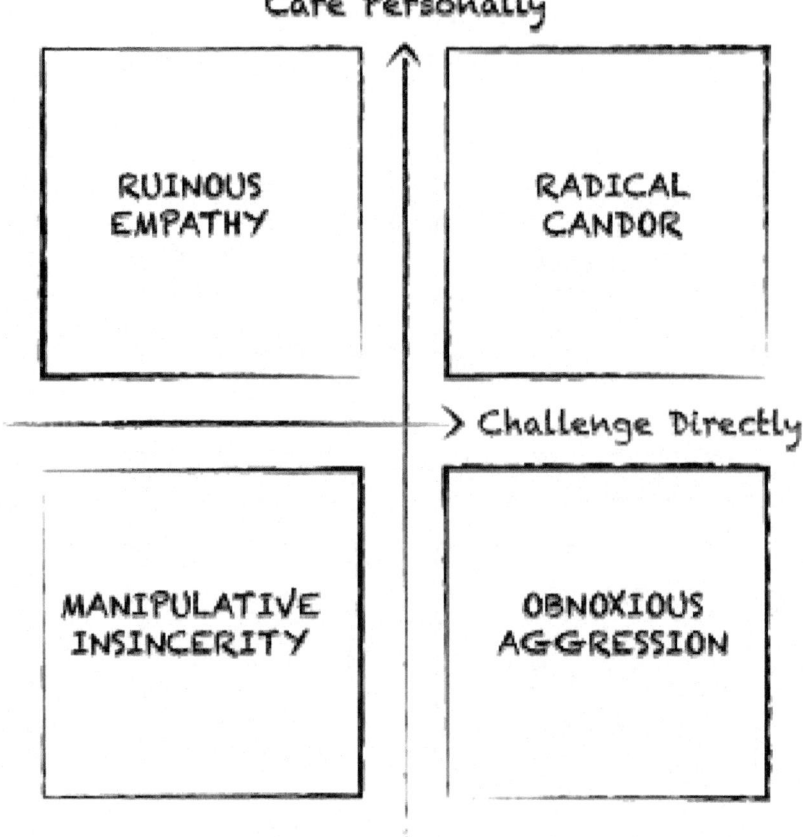

"Most managerial errors occur due to 'ruinous empathy,' where leaders care about their workers but do not challenge them. These managers don't *give the constructive criticism that their employees need to improve,"* says Kim.

Ruinous empathy is the most common form: I care about you and don't want to offend you, so I don't tell you that your dress doesn't look good, your word choices could be misunderstood, or your work could be better. In practice, I am lying to you.

#THE MIND LIES

Just as when we don't open ourselves up to others, it is impossible to establish an authentic and mutually sustainable connection. Every time we lie, omit, or disguise feedback, the relationship we are building begins to falter. The knots loosen, eventually unraveling, and one knot after another, our network collapses.

The mind lies[18], and it lies to us too. In practice, it deceives us using biases and heuristics[19] to make judgments, which then become prejudices about things we have never seen or have no experience of.

A prejudice comes before having the elements to make a judgment and distorts it.

In the 1960s, a group of researchers led by Robert Rosenthal conducted an experiment to demonstrate the weight of prejudices and their effect on students' performance.

They administered an IQ test to children and then gave the results to the teachers, stating that a particular group was brilliant. One year later, Rosenthal demonstrated that positive prejudices had led to excellent results, while negative biases had hindered the performance of other children. The teachers treated the children differently based on the initial prejudice (high IQ, low IQ). It's a shame that the tests were manipulated, disrupting the data.

This experiment shows us that perception triumphs over reality and that prejudice compromises facts.

Take a bad grade in math (or art, or on a short essay in second grade), and for the rest of our lives, we hate the subject, can't

---

[18] "La mente mente"https://www.amazon.it/mente-siamo-quando-nessuno-guarda/dp/8895369351

[19] Heuristics are mental tricks that lead to quick conclusions with minimal cognitive effort.

understand it, and continue to worsen.

Conversely, confirmation from a long time ago brings long-term benefits.

The belief that just because someone is well-known, they will never respond to you is a product of living with prejudices. Almost thirty years ago, when YouTube did not yet exist and the internet was taking its first steps, I searched for a song my mother often sang to remember her father, "o Mein Papà." My father loved playing the piano and desperately searched for the version played with the trumpet by Nini Rosso [20] in MIDI [21] format to delight the family with music and singing. I searched for Nini Rosso in a thousand ways, and finally, I found an email and wrote to him. The emotion I felt when I saw the response in my inbox was indescribable. Not only because it was a time when an email was not an everyday occurrence but also because such a famous and relevant figure for my parents took the trouble to respond, saying, "I'm sorry, but there is no MIDI version." He passed away a year later, in 1994.

Confirmation Bias is the prejudice that fuels our viewpoint and strengthens it.

If Siri (so important to me and recognized by the world) asked the same question and asked others, then I am on the right track.

Group Bias leads us to overestimate the abilities and value of our community, those like us, and conversely, to distrust everyone else.

Our family is better than the others in the building.

Our city is nicer than the one just a half-mile away.

Italians do it best: Italians believe they're the best in the world at making ... pizza.

Germans who claim to be the best at making sauerkraut.

The French ARE the best.

From biases to stereotypes, the step is short, indeed immediate.

All men are jerks, and all women are pink.
But "Italians first" and "go back to your country."

When evaluating a person or a situation, if we associate them with

---

[20] https://youtu.be/ewBVkPdTGw0

[21] https://it.wikipedia.org/wiki/Musical_Instrument_Digital_Interface

someone or something we have seen in the past, we are slipping into the so-called **Gabler fallacy** (named after the theorist who coined it to avoid forgetting it).

The first impression is what counts.

When I was still in law school (for an extended period) and also doing consulting work, I had a nose piercing - a small silver dot on my right nostril -and if I must say so, I wore it with a certain decent nonchalance. Just after graduating, when I entered the law firm where I would practice law, I had to remove the tiny sparkle from my nose because it was deemed inappropriate for professional attire. Needless to ignore this fact: for most people, appearances matter.

On another continent, America, in another setting—a communal kitchen in a university dorm, like the ones we see in movies—A guy is washing dishes and utensils. Upon seeing him, I thought he was from the African continent. As the program manager in which he participated as a student, I tried to create an empathetic connection through an ironic remark about Americans' poor hygiene in kitchens. It was an international program involving more than 40 countries, and I assumed he was not American. Okay, you get it. He looked at me perplexed, understanding my blunder. Should we keep going down the path of blindly following stereotypes?

When we perceive someone in another person as familiar, we are inclined to overestimate that person due to the resemblance:

The Projection Bias resembles the similarity bias (!): even though we all feel unique, we think that most people think like us and, consequently, behave like us.

This bias correlates with the **false consensus**, in which we believe others think like and agree with us.

The Present Bias, or *hyperbolic discounting*, makes us choose the chicken instead of the egg: I'm hungry now, and I eat; we'll see later. And in the context of relationships, it is extremely important since it influences at least three areas of our lives: food, savings, and work.

There are too many biases to discuss in this context, but it is sufficient to know that the **status quo bias** is linked to resistance to change; **the PeacockBbias** (self-enhancing transmission bias) makes us more likely to share successes rather than failures. Just look at Instagram: a universe of people on cloud nine, all beautiful, all happy, and content. **The omission bias** leads us to inaction, even when our lives are in danger.

We don't choose for fear of making the wrong choice.

Ritov and Baron demonstrated this by telling some parents about a deadly epidemic and asking them if they would vaccinate their children or not. Faced with uncertainty, the majority of subjects opposed vaccination.
Sounds familiar?
Uncertainties are often accepted as truths when spread by social media. At some point, we must rely on common sense. In a global pandemic, despite all the questionable metrics—from how infections and deaths are calculated globally to the effectiveness of a vaccine that couldn't undergo standard verification—we should rely on and follow common sense.

On the other hand, **Action Biases**, the last ones I promise, are the opposite of Omission Biases: we act when we shouldn't, like a goalkeeper who knows they should stay centered but can't help moving around.

FROM BIASES TO ERRORS

The issue with biases is that they cause us to make arbitrary decisions, which in turn leads to mistakes.

Psychiatrist Aaron Beck, who founded cognitive therapy, proposed a model where mood disorders stem from evaluation errors that are influenced by patterns established early in our lives. These errors can be grouped (again: schematized) into ten behaviors.

1. Jumping to conclusions
Drawing a foregone conclusion from an analysis of a situation, regardless of the lack of evidence or even in the face of contradicting evidence. We messaged Maria, but since she hadn't read our message, we deduced that she wouldn't respond because she was not interested.

2. Playing the Oracle
Predicting the future with certainty (e.g., "I will have a panic attack if I go to that supermarket").

3. Focusing only on the negatives, not the positives
Selective abstraction, adverse selection.

Nine out of ten things may go right, but we obsess over the one thing that doesn't.

4. Earthquake and tragedy
If Maria doesn't respond, I should stop writing to anyone.
Just because she didn't respond doesn't mean no one will.
I'll never find another job.
I'll end up living under a bridge.

5. Personalizing
Maria didn't read my message because it was from me.
Maria (who didn't read my message) wrote on Twitter that she was angry; she must definitely be mad at me; it's my fault.

6. All or nothing
Dichotomizing everything as either all or nothing: not allowing for intermediate possibilities (e.g., "if I don't do the job perfectly, it's worthless").

7. Painting everyone with the same broad brush
Regarding others:
If Maria didn't respond to me, it's because she's stuck up.
Regarding ourselves:
I couldn't get Maria to respond, so I'm incapable of networking.

8. Making judgements based on emotions
Believing emotions reflect facts (e.g., "I feel anxious, so there must be a threat").
I don't feel like writing to her, so it's better not to because if I'm anxious, there must be a reason...

9. Telepathy
Reading minds is not (yet) possible but creating scenarios about what we believe others are thinking is commonplace.
Maria didn't respond to me because she thinks I'm not up to her standards.

10. Magnifying/minimizing
Exaggerating or diminishing the importance of events or situations. Minimizing is a process similar to "devaluation," where positive experiences are not considered because they lack value.

Aaron Beck gives patients a sheet that lists and describes each of these cognitive distortions. The patient then marks the processes they recognize as their own and describes situations in which they have used those distorted processes. In practice, therapy essentially involves training in logical thinking.

*

So it was then that the fox appeared.

"Good morning," said the fox.

"Good morning," replied the little prince politely, turning around but not seeing anyone.

"I'm here," said the voice, "under the apple tree."

"Who are you?" asked the little prince. "You are gorgeous..."

"I am a fox," said the fox.

"Come and play with me," proposed the little prince. "I am so sad..."

"I cannot play with you," answered the fox. "I am not tamed."

"Oh, I'm sorry," said the little prince.

But after thinking about it, he added: "What does 'tamed' mean?"

"You are not from around here," said the fox. "What are you looking for?"

"I am looking for men," replied the little prince. "What does 'tamed' mean?"

"Men," said the fox, "they have guns, and they hunt. That isn't very pleasant! They also raise chickens. That is their only interest. Are you looking for chickens?"

"No," said the little prince. "I am looking for friends. What does 'tamed' mean?"

"It is an act that is unfortunately forgotten," answered the fox. "It means 'to establish ties...'"

"To establish ties?"

"Certainly," said the fox. "To me, you are just a little boy, like a hundred thousand other little boys. I don't need you. And you don't need me either. To you, I am just a fox like a hundred thousand others. But if you tame me, we shall need each other. You will be unique to me in all the world. And I shall be unique to you..."

"I begin to understand," said the little prince. "There is a flower... I think she has tamed me..."

TAME - DOMESTICATE

Domesticating means making something familiar, which is exactly what the fox and the Little Prince do for each other: they form a connection, a link in a network.

Fourteen thousand years BCE, we domesticated the wolves[22]; 13,000 years ago, the bees; 8,000 years ago, goats, sheep, and pigs; 10,000 years ago, cows. Starting in the 1930s, we domesticated hamsters, and in the 1970s, in Sweden, we even succeeded with deer.

Meanwhile, we did the same with plants, which we used to forage across continents, moving on after depleting local resources in search of new areas to exploit. We then began farming in the Fertile Crescent (including areas in modern-day Palestine, Jordan, Syria, and Egypt).

Over the millennia, we've learned to tame wild animals to suit our needs, preferences, and even current trends. Throughout our history, we've also evolved our tastes, learning to appreciate things like foods, scents, drinks, and phenomena that we once found repulsive or incomprehensible.

The fact that we've successfully domesticated both horses and our own taste preferences suggests that we also have a good chance of bettering ourselves by understanding and adapting the mechanisms and systems that govern us.

How?

---

[22] But perhaps it domesticated itself, as a 2015 study by the University of Aberdeen, Scotland, showed:
- https://www.sciencemag.org/news/2015/04/feature-solving-mystery-dog-domestication

https://science.sciencemag.org/content/348/6232/274.full

Thanks to a four-point plan that—surprise—all start with the letter 'P,' which also stands for People, Planet, Profit, and of course, Purpose.

1. Pacing 2. Practice
3. Pleasure 4. More Pleasure (Amplifying pleasure).

A PROJECT FOR SELF-TAMING

We can call it a plan, a project, a program, or even a list. Whether you jot it down on paper, in a locked diary like the ones I used in the '90s, or digitally in a smartphone app, the key is to visualize it and then make it happen.

In other words, make it tangible, something you can print out and touch if you wanted to, without this P of ours turn into another self-imposed trap, or a cage.

What we really need is not just a list, but a roadmap that takes us from where we are today to where we want to be tomorrow. In creating this map, our minds don't just focus on the journey; they start to visualize the destination.

As we articulate our PURPOSE, we pause and look ahead, already envisioning the future scenario we want for ourselves. At the very moment when the retina acquires and processes the information, our brain is already producing hormones that help us in the process.

#1. 'P' FOR PACING

The brain is plastic. Taming is possible, but it's not a walk in the park, and it takes time, willingness, and consistency. A lot, a whole lot of consistency.

"But I'm in a rush."

I know we're all pressed for time, with hours that seem to fly by. In our constant rush, we've convinced ourselves that we don't have time, especially not for self-improvement. However, in order to tame our brain, to remove, one by one, the layers that the world, society, and ourselves have sewn onto us, we must necessarily find it.

We must give ourselves the time to approach change gradually. We must give our brain time to get used to not judging, not boxing people in, or categorizing them. We must give ourselves the time, and the space, to shed all those constructions that limit us. We must self-tame calmly, one step at a time, to learn to be more open to others and thus be able to build valuable relationships and networks.

And to succeed, we cannot be in a hurry.

The famous seven kilograms in seven days is a trap disguised as a myth that has allowed the sale of several million copies of crash diet books and just as many, if not more, courses and related products. But these books and courses only work sometimes: at best, when we undergo diets, as well as any other attempt to change quickly, we end up exactly where we started, if not a little further behind.

Pyramids were built one stone at a time, and the world's tallest peaks were scaled inch by inch.

The best and most lasting changes in business productivity come in small steps. The Japanese philosophy KAIZEN also says so, which forms the basis of Total Quality Control Management that, even today, almost half a century later, continues to allow the reduction of errors in the production process.

The Kaizen Mode[23]l can be helpful to us for all five of its S's.

1. Seiri - Choose and Separate. Eliminate anything unnecessary in the workspace.

2. Seiton - Organize and arrange. Efficiently organize tools, equipment, materials, etc.

3. Seison - Check the created order and cleanliness.

4. Seiketsu - Standardize and improve. Maintain the created order and cleanliness, and continuously seek improvement by repeating the steps: Seiri, Seiton, Seison.

5. Shitsuke - Sustain over time. Impose discipline and rigor for the future.

What do lean manufacturing principles have to do with networking, and how can they help us?

When we free ourselves from the superfluous and everything that hinders us, we can see the essential and therefore organize it better with SEITON (stability), which allows us to find the suitable spaces, times, and tools, which we then have to keep CLEAN (SEISO), maintained, and continuously improved (SHITSUKE).

This is where our second "P" stands for small steps, repeated and

---

[23] In Japanese Seiri, Seiton, Seison, Seiketsu, Shitsuke; in English: Sort, Set in Order, Shine, Standardize, Sustain.

continuously improved.

I want to connect with X, so I make myself visible while keeping a respectful distance, much like the Little Prince did with the fox. If I were to get too close, I would risk scaring X, who might even think I'm stalking them.

As I make contact from a distance, I begin to understand who this person is, I read what they write, how they communicate, what they do, etc.

I have already formed a personal connection: the person in question may not yet know it, but from my perspective, they have already ceased to be distant (and therefore somewhat unattainable and scary).

Then I take another small step, and instead of appearing in their mailbox or private messages, I start showing up where they hang out.

So I wait, giving this fledgling connection—a seedling of a relationship—the chance to grow. When the person sees me, responds to, or approves my comment, I can take another step to get closer. But even if they don't do it explicitly (with a like or a response), there's a good chance they have seen me, and consequently, I am no longer a complete stranger to this person.

"If you can't fly, then run. If you can't run, then walk. If you can't walk, then crawl. But whatever you do, you have to keep moving forward."
Martin Luther King Jr.

#2. 'P' FOR PRACTICE, PERPETUATION

The second 'P' stands for practice, specifically repetition, a concept closely related to taming (which we've already discussed), training, and conditioning (which we'll discuss shortly).

We all know how to repeat things, and sometimes we do it excessively without truly understanding what we're repeating. Whether it's passing on information we just heard, memorizing a poem in second grade, or learning articles of the Constitution for a law exam, repetition is key. We also use it to remember names to avoid embarrassment or to establish certain gestures, patterns, and behaviors.

We learn to speak through repetition: we hear a sound and try to mimic it until it sounds the same.

Similarly, by repeating, we learn a language, a sport, or a set of skills because observation alone is not enough to acquire an ability. To make it our own, whatever capacity it may be, we need to repeat it.

It works for tennis, crocheting, and balance sheets, and it also works for communication, the art of connecting with other human beings and establishing a relationship that supports all parties involved.

One attempt follows another. One iteration after the next. This approach also applies to innovation and all of human discovery. We might have discovered fire by accident, but taming it likely required an ancestor spending hours—possibly even entire lunar cycles—repeating the same action until it became second nature.

"Owning a net isn't sufficient to catch butterflies; you need practice, patience, skill, and a little luck."
(Olivia Fox Cabane)[24]

o network effectively, practice is more important than charisma. Theory is helpful, but it's not sufficient. To build and maintain a strong network, we need to keep repeating the same actions until they become second nature—until they feel neither strange nor forced but instead familiar and natural. This will lead to positive outcomes that fuel a virtuous cycle of satisfaction.

#3. 'P' FOR PLEASURE

What does pleasure have to do with networking ability? It matters because pleasure is the fuel of that machine we call the brain, and depending on how much pleasure it has in its tank, it either propels us into action or keeps us glued to the couch—or to our device screens, which is essentially the same thing.

Networking doesn't have a formula, but humans do. In a way,

---

[24] Olivia Fox Cabane, the best-selling author of The Charisma Myth, was director of innovative leadership at Stanford's StartX, where Judah Pollack was also a faculty member. He lectures at UC Berkeley's Haas School of Business.

before we are lawyers, networkers, or even people, we are walking chemical reactions.

We're walking chemical reactions because, as NASA asserts, life itself is a self-sustaining, self-replicating chemical system that aligns with Charles Darwin's theories of evolution.

We're born from a chemical reaction and live under the sway of chemical processes that can make us happy, incredibly sad, ready to run, poised for battle, fired up, or just plain apathetic—even to the point of not wanting to eat. Chemical reactions govern us; most of the time, they do so without us realizing it. Some reactions work against us, paralyzing us, while others fill us with energy.

DOPAMINE

Dopamine, for example, is the neurotransmitter of pleasure and reward. Also known as the hormone of euphoria, dopamine is released when we experience pleasure. Besides making us feel great, it is also responsible for sleep, personal motivation (because it predicts the reward even before completing something), memory, learning, and even muscles.

We feel down, demotivated, and apathetic when dopamine levels are low. When they are high, we are on cloud nine.

Since the dopamine levels in our system determine our mood and productivity (with the former directly influencing the latter), we would be tempted to consume dopamine like a spoonful, just like we can do with serotonin, which increases with chocolate and good sex. Unfortunately, we cannot do the same with dopamine because the endogenous one, naturally produced within our body, cannot be directly assimilated orally. Although no dopamine pills are available yet, there are some ways to help our body produce it.

Such as?

Certain foods boost levels of two hormones—phenylalanine and tyrosine—that are precursors to dopamine. Foods like wheat germ, legumes, meat, eggs, and fish are rich in phenylalanine. Meanwhile, nuts, bananas, avocados, oily seeds like sesame, pumpkin, and sunflower, as well as dairy products, cocoa, and turmeric are rich in tyrosine. Physical activity helps, too: Just 30 to 40 minutes of walking a day can stimulate dopamine production. Music is also a potent dopamine booster, even comparable to sex.

Every time we achieve a goal we set for ourselves, dopamine is produced. Moreover, even before reaching the goal, our body releases dopamine, and it almost acts as a self-fulfilling prophecy, predicting the sensation we will experience (the chemical reward). It helps us overcome obstacles and, in a word, succeed. Friendship and relationships, in general, are also a source of dopamine and laughter.

SEROTONIN

Serotonin is a natural substance that functions as a neurotransmitter, carrying signals between neurons - the nerve cells - throughout the body.

In the brain, it helps regulate mood and memory. It involves sleep, sex, libido, bone health, and blood clotting. In the gut - where 95% of our serotonin is produced - it facilitates and promotes digestion[25].

The fact that serotonin is mainly produced in the gut tells us how important our gut is for our well-being. With our gut, we can feel certain things and even instinctively evaluate them. When we say, "I feel it in my gut," we talk about positive and negative emotions. And yet, this is not just a figure of speech because, for several years now, the relationship between mood states and the gut microbiota (our bacterial flora, an army that lives with us and regulates a significant part of our lives) has been demonstrated by Michael D. Gershon, who decided to rename the gut as the "second brain" (and did so with a book[26] that immediately became a bestseller). The definition is mainly symbolic because there are around 500 million neurons in the gut, while the brain has over 85 billion, but it helps us see how much the gut matters in our lives. It tells us that how we eat, what we eat, and especially how much we eat, influences how we feel, our mood, and therefore our relationships with others.

OXYTOCIN

Oxytocin is known as the "love hormone." Females of all mammalian species produce it after giving birth to facilitate bonding with their offspring and breastfeeding. It is also the hormone that all of

---

[25] https://www.technologynetworks.com/neuroscience/news/how-serotonin-balances-communication-in-the-brain-333198]

[26] "The second brain doesn't help with the great thought processes...religion, philosophy and poetry is left to the brain in the head," says Michael Gershon, chairman of the Department of Anatomy and Cell Biology at New York–Presbyterian Hospital/Columbia University Medical Center, an expert in the nascent field of neurogastroenterology and author of the 1998 book *The Second Brain* (HarperCollins).

us produce during orgasm. Produced by the pituitary gland and released by specific cell receptors through the bloodstream, oxytocin helps us empathize, form bonds, and maintain them over the long term.

It has been shown[27] that a spray of oxytocin in the nose makes people more open to relationships, more available, and even better at recognizing others' emotions. This happens because the inhibitory brakes of the prefrontal and cortico-limbic circuits are lowered. Furthermore, oxytocin promotes sociability - and therefore networking - and even monogamy.

Regarding sociability, researchers at the Max Planck Institute for Evolutionary Anthropology in Leipzig, Germany, studied the ability to form long-term cooperative relationships by examining 26 chimpanzees from the Budongo Forest in Uganda. By measuring their oxytocin levels, they discovered that the hormone varied depending on the type of activity the chimpanzees were engaged in: it was lower during grooming operations and significantly higher during food sharing.

When it comes to fidelity, a study published in The Journal of Neuroscience shows that oxytocin boosts loyalty by reducing the likelihood of betrayal.

#4. THE PLEASURE 'P'

Is there an error?

Is it repetitive or perhaps a typographical error?

No, there is no error. The fifth 'P' in this process of self-domestication is once again 'Pleasure'. Because the hormones we mentioned in the previous pages are the cornerstone of human productivity and our successes.

Dopamine, serotonin, oxytocin, and endorphins can aid us in our networking efforts. They can influence how others perceive us and can either positively or negatively impact our well-being. Understanding how they work and learning to regulate their balance naturally helps us not only to "feel better" but, first and foremost, Free ourselves from the burdens that otherwise restrict our actions and their corresponding outcomes.

---

[27] " https://www.psicologiapositiva.it/ossitocina/]

To *domesticate* our brain, we must know it. It is unnecessary (although it would help) to obtain a degree in medicine and specialize in neuroscience. Still, it is enough to do some research and then start paying attention to how we feel at a specific moment (as well as how we have felt).

Just recalling an achievement is enough to reproduce feelings of well-being and stimulate the production of the respective hormones.

Just thinking about a goal is enough for dopamine to kick in.

Just remembering someone we love is enough to trigger oxytocin.

This is not magic and has nothing to do with new-age philosophies of "imagine-you-can." It's just chemistry, and how it works with us (and for us or against us) also works for other people.

"The basic chemistry of all living organisms is the same, from the simplest bacteria to humans."
Mario Ageno

TRAIN

According to the Assalco Report 2020[28], there are three hundred million pets in Europe and over sixty million in Italy, averaging one pet for every resident. If we exclude fish, which make up almost half of the total and are not easily trainable, in that case, we have learned to interact with other animals, realizing that certain things work and others that don't: if Jack, the Russell terrier, brings us the ball and we give him a treat, he will continue to get it back and do it even better; conversely, if he fails and we scold him, he will never learn.

Rewards encourage animals, while punishment, such as a bad grade or criticism, diminishes their desire to perform. But rewards not only motivate dogs, cats, ducks, and Bengal tigers: **recognition encourages all living beings**, starting from a pair of communicating cells. Therefore, our brain, as well as that of all other multicellular organisms, is trainable. In practice, it is capable of changing and acquiring skills even in activities that were previously unknown to us.

As early as 1906, an Italian scientist named Ernesto Lugaro[29] used the term "brain plasticity," which has since entered the common language.

---

[28] Assalco: Associazione Nazionale Imprese per l'Alimentazione e la cura degli animali da Compagnia

[29] Berlucchi G (2002) The origin of the term plasticity in the neurosciences: Ernesto Lugaro and chemical synaptic transmission. J Hist Neurosci 11:305–309

"During my travels, I met a scientist who enabled people blind from birth to start seeing; I spoke with patients who had been declared incurable after suffering a stroke decades earlier. But were helped to recover through neuroplastic treatments. I met people who overcame learning disorders and improved their own. I gathered evidence that at eighty years old, it is possible to make the memory more vibrant so that it functions as it did at fifty-five.

I have seen patients 'rewire' their brains through thoughts, resolving traumas and obsessions previously considered insurmountable."

Norman Doidge[30]

If our brains are plastic, we can embrace the necessary changes to free ourselves from the constructs we've imposed on ourselves. We can train it, just as we do with puppies, to learn to break free from prejudices, to open up to others, and to help us build relationships and connections that benefit all parties involved.

How?
Through training. 😊

---

[30] Norman Doigde, researcher at the Columbia University Psychoanalytic Center in New York and the department of psychiatry at the University of Toronto, and author of the bestseller "The Brain That Changes Itself (2008)

COACHING

We are accustomed to thinking of training as something athletes do to prepare for a competition, beat a record, win a medal, and make their fans happy. We define training as an activity that requires consistent planning and repetition. We train our bodies to stay fit or achieve what they say we should have: we train our glutes, chest muscles, and even the facial muscles discovered by Instagram in recent years. We train for endurance, to handle fatigue, and to learn new languages. We train our memory. We train to speak publicly, to step onto a stage, and to put on a performance. And every time we train, we make a series of efforts: before starting, to find motivation, and during, to maintain focus on what we're doing and, above all, not to give up. To maintain momentum — known as 'lena' in archaic Italian.

"And like one who, with the weary breath, has reached the shore after swimming in the sea."[31]

The term 'lena' is derived from the Italian word 'anelare,' which means to breathe forcefully and vigorously. We struggle, sweat, and suffer. We experience and endure pain, but throughout each training minute, we are focused on the reps, the miles, the yellow tennis balls on the red court, and the goal posts at the end of the track. And this happens to everyone, to Andre Agassi and Federica Brignone alike.

This applies to weekend cyclists and ultra-runners alike, such as Daniele Barbone. At one point in his career as an eco-entrepreneur, he

---

[31] «E come quei che con lena affannata uscito fuor del pelago a la riva»

took up running without prior experience and quickly tackled the Big Five—the planet's five most challenging marathons—as well as the 100-kilometer Sahara Desert run and the insect-laden Amazon race.

However, no one would do it if training were solely about enduring pain. The truth is that movement stimulates the production of well-being hormones, and while fatigue hurts on the one hand, it makes us feel better on the other.

Just as we train our bodies, we can train our brains to *rewire* entire areas, teaching a specific zone to take on the role of another (neuroscientists call this "brain plasticity"). Similarly, we can train ourselves to shed our inherent biases that hold us back, moving beyond the comfortable but limiting beliefs that prevent us from being truly open with others.

We can train ourselves to build valuable relationships, freeing ourselves from labels, the fear of rejection, common notions about networking, the illusion of talent, and the storytelling of so-called mind-readers.

GET RID OF...

#1. LABELS

No boxes, no prejudice.

To build a valuable relationship, we must strip ourselves of the tendency to classify people, judging them before even listening to them.

We must learn to be open.

To establish a positive connection, it's important to empathize with the other person and share their emotions. To really put ourselves in someone else's shoes, we should approach them gradually and be open to listening. If I want to get to know Maria, I need to approach her world with the same kindness as the Little Prince from Saint-Exupéry. I should take it one step at a time and one day at a time. Without rushing, I can learn about her space and understand who she is, what interests her, and what scares her.

Even if digital identity doesn't always coincide with confirmed identity, by frequenting *her environments*, I will still have the opportunity to listen to her, read what she writes (what she posts and comments on), and reflect on the most familiar language. I will begin to know her, even from a distance, long before I write to her.

We always start with how she appears, what she posts, which profile photos she chooses, how many interactions she has and how often, which contacts we have in common, her work experience, and her interests.

Labels, tags, and hashtags are frameworks we create. They help define who we are through what we choose to share. If we decide not to be present on social media, we also convey a clear message: a lack of interest in positioning our brand. This is somewhat of an outdated choice, especially since LinkedIn accounts for 60% of job opportunities. But in any case, we accept it.

But why the search for a label? Why the need to position ourselves with our own identity?

The need to be recognizable stems from the fateful question: what will I do when I grow up? And an answer to this fateful question must be given. "Must" because everyone expects it: family, school, friends, society as a whole. As the years go by, we become adults and then grown-ups. We make choices, and in some way, we become those choices. We open a profile on LinkedIn to connect with other links in the same chain.

People need to quickly recognize and categorize us. Therefore, we need some sort of 'costume' to present ourselves to the world. This costume identifies us at first glance and immediately tells us who we are. Hence, from one year to another, lawyer, accountant, and designer are no longer enough: skills are needed, all the skills, and if possible, even certificates: Web Strategies, certified Google ADS, SEM specialist, ADV Specialist, Growth hacking, Web Analyst, E-commerce Manager, and so on. But algorithms change, and even certificates are no longer enough to stand out at some point: a distinguishing phrase[32] is needed. Like the ones below, the brands and trademarks once called "slogans" are now pay-offs or taglines.

Where there's Barilla, there's home.
Think different.
Just Do It!
I'm lovin' it

In practice, a line below our name on LinkedIn and other social media **should** summarize our brand and display our slogan to those who might need us. That's what the gurus of personal branding taught us, right? Exactly, but this costume that makes us recognizable—or at least attempts to—is the same one that installs all the biases we discussed in the previous chapters.

The label we sew onto ourselves to be accepted is the same one that categorizes us and confines us to a specific cluster: that of lawyers and accountants, but also the cluster of title collectors, those who try to be

---

[32] https://www.coburgbanks.co.uk/blog/friday-funnies/50-hilarious-linkedin-headlines/

funny at all costs, sellers of hot air. And the same principle applies not just to ourselves, but also to how we perceive others.

Shedding these labels, and not placing too much importance on others' labels, is crucial for building valuable relationships. These can start as simple connections and potentially develop into friendships.

#2. FEAR OF BEING REJECTED

Another layer we need to get rid of is the fear of rejection. We must stop trembling at the thought of someone ignoring us or saying no. Deep down, we've been used to hearing 'no' since childhood. It's normal to be told no, but as we grow up, especially when we tell ourselves that we have "made it" (whatever that means), a no becomes much scarier.

However, a no is not a failure, just like a failure is not a zombie apocalypse. A no is simply a no. It may sound obvious, almost banal, but it's ridiculously accurate, like all tautologies, which are statements true by definition. Do you remember Boskov, the great Serbian soccer player who became a coach, and his memorable sayings? Many of them are precisely tautologies and, as such, impossible to dismantle.

"Those who don't shoot at the goal don't score" is undoubtedly a truism, a prominent and indisputable truth, not only in football. Similarly, "The ball is ours, we play; the ball is theirs, they play" or "The game is over when the referee blows the whistle."

Furthermore, there's no final whistle when it comes to networking and human relationships. The game is open-ended, without deadlines, because real networking work spans a lifetime, not just 90 minutes or a few days. To build lasting and mutually beneficial connections, we need to understand that it's not a sprint but a marathon; we don't need to race against the clock, but rather invest time and care.

You can't build bridges at the 'last minute,' especially not ones that will stand the test of time.

Networking is about farming, not hunting." — Ivan Misner, founder of BNI International.

3. COLLECTION OF CONTACTS

We touched on this earlier in this booklet: the networking world is filled with clichés, one of which is the idea that a network is only valid, meaning it's only considered effective, reasonable, or profitable if it is significant.

The networking that makes us grow is not a directory; it is not a collection of names and data to show off (to whom?) or, even worse, to exploit when convenient. It is a constructive approach that should be integrated into our lives.

A good network cannot be too vast either, or the quality of the connections will inevitably decrease, becoming weaker. You need to actively nurture and maintain the network: if there are too many elements, we will need more time for everyone.

Some specialize in network marketing. Having a list of contacts is crucial in that field to expand the business I'll be the first to admit that I've fallen for the allure of network marketing not just once, but twice. The person who roped me in was skilled in making me feel important and valuing me when their interest was only the quantity of contacts I brought along. I even went so far as to invest money in buying beauty products, and I begrudgingly paid a monthly fee to restock them. I should feel ashamed to tell you this, but if you've reached this point in the book, it means you have found positive elements for reflection. So if you have a large contact list, think twice before diving into network marketing. They are interested in who you know more than in you.

#4. ILLUSION OF TALENT

To build a valuable network, you don't need to be talented. You don't even need to be extroverted. In practice, you don't need a specific talent; even if you did, we have already seen how skills can be cultivated. Some people are born with one, none, or a hundred thousand talents, and then they waste them, burying them in the ground, out of reach from thieves, just like in the similar parable. And there are those who build and refine their talents and then manage to profit from them.

We have already discussed this regarding training and practice: the brain is 'plastic,' or malleable, and it is up to us to teach it how to react.

> *"Every artist was first an amateur."*
> — Ralph Waldo Emerson

On the contrary, the illusion that talent is necessary to establish sustainable relationships only limits our movements.

#5. MIND-READERS

Since the late 1980s, we have been bombarded with information and NLP (Neuro-Linguistic Programming) courses and programs that provide bullet-point format lessons taught—and mostly sold—by life coaches who present themselves as masters of life. This is what "life coach" means.

In the 1400s, the word "coach" only referred to a carriage. In the 19th century, it was used for tutors at English universities whose task was (and still is) to help students finish their studies. In the last two decades of the 20th century, it was adopted by sports coaches who guide professionals in achieving their goals. From there, it gained traction and proliferated, moving beyond the playing field and entering the business world first and then our homes. Their purpose is no longer to help us win a game but to guide us in all the games we decide to play.

"I tell you to jump, and you jump."

The success of motivators like Anthony Robbins has led to the multiplication of coaches and aspiring coaches and the proliferation of a new army of self-entrepreneurs who saw Tony Robbins as an easy way to make money at the expense of the vulnerable. I realize my stance may be unpopular, but it's informed by the stories I've heard of dozens of people who approached this world full of hope only to find themselves in debt with zero results.

The narrative is powerful and calibrated to attract and make us believe in mantras like "if you want, you can" whatever it takes. The coaching universe has a storytelling approach full of essential references and high-profile connections: from Socrates' maieutics (the art of helping minds give birth) to neuroscience and studies from numerous universities. It is also filled with examples, so-called facts that we more or less all know, which are presented to demonstrate this or that theory. Steve Jobs started in a garage. So did Jeff Bezos. Einstein had terrible grades. Faraday needed to learn the language of mathematics. And so on. But like any good story, interest starts to fade and needs to be rekindled after some time. That's when the 'anti-gurus,' or coaches who are critical of traditional coaching, emerge, along with other texts that explain why coaching (typically "coaching as done by others") doesn't work.

In the end, no matter how you look at it, it is still a form of conditioning, and personally - and here I return to my uncomfortable position - I don't appreciate those who try to condition me or others.

Returning to communication, language can be strategic, purposeful, effective, negotiable, and much more, but it should never be conditioning or conditioned. And certainly not intentionally.

Effective communication, the kind that allows us to form genuine relationships, has nothing to do with conditioning and/or NLP; it is not manipulation, a trick, or a trap. It's speaking clearly, and honestly without beating around the bush while respecting the other person. Being assertive is all about speaking your mind clearly and respectfully. So, just two things: clarity and respect. If we can let go of the hype spun by over-the-top salespeople and ignore the exaggerated claims and supposed 'mind-reading' tactics. In that case, we are free to build an authentic connection with other people, one at a time, and from that point on, we can start building a network that's actually sustainable.

GET USED TO...

And so, please, what does it take to build a valuable network? To create a network of sustainable relationships?

It takes time, empathy, active listening, preparation, assertiveness, care, and enjoyment.

#1. EMPATHY

What is empathy?

According to Treccani, an authoritative Italian dictionary:

Empathy, or 'empatìa' in Italian, is a term that originates from the Greek words "ἐν" (in) and "-patia." It is analogous to the German word 'Einfühlung.' In psychology, it generally refers to the ability to understand another person's emotional state and situation immediately, mostly without resorting to verbal communication.

What is empathy for? It helps simplify both professional and personal relationships by making it easier to exchange opinions, resolve conflicts, and manage relationships at all levels. It allows us to put ourselves in the shoes - and in the pathos - of the other person.

How does empathy help us in the workplace?

It narrows the gap, breaks down prejudices, and overcomes biases, bringing us closer to others. Sure, an architect can design a house alone, but when they empathize with the future homeowner before starting the design, their work is more meaningful.

Empathy is the ability to put oneself in someone else's shoes and, concretely, to feel what they are experiencing. This does not necessarily mean that the other person understands our own processes. On the contrary, an empathic connection is precisely a one-way journey: from us to the other person.

Relationships built on the foundations of empathic connection are the most solid.

Let's start with the assumption that building relationships is an act of generosity. We give attention, time, and willingness to share skills and experiences. But the other person doesn't need to do the same because we are secondary: what matters is our interlocutor.

This point is crucial: every time we put ourselves in the background, the other person becomes the center of our attention, and they know it; this will lead them to open up to us.

It may happen that they can't enter our emotional sphere, but this is not by chance. We are the ones who empathize, facilitate the exchange, and build valuable relationships for mutual benefit. We're not necessarily trying to make friends or find 'soulmates' in brief networking or business encounters. Our initial goal is to build a positive relationship.

The other person unconsciously appreciates the opportunity to talk about themselves and what they do. However, it often happens that when that potential networking relationship turns into a friendship (which is natural after getting to know each other better), I hear them say, "I didn't think you were like this."

It happens to me often.

What does "like this" mean, I wonder? So, I ask for explanations. The response I received was that I seemed distant at first, focused more on listening and less on sharing.

Indeed, I am inclined toward an "empathetic" mode, to the extent that the people who have said to me, "I didn't think you were like this," are those who started a business relationship with me before becoming friends.

Mission accomplished.

#2. ACTIVE LISTENING

To succeed in building a positive relationship through empathy, there are some steps that can help achieve this goal.

First, let's begin by putting ourselves in the other person's shoes: we start from their perspective, not ours. The person we're talking to is more important than we are at that specific moment. Let's imagine that our words could change the destiny of the person we are talking to. The strength of this sentiment will be reflected in our terms, creating an immediate empathic connection.

While observing the person speaking to us, we maintain a calm expression with a slight closed-lip smile without losing eye contact to demonstrate that we are engaged, give them the attention they deserve, and are happy to be where we are. At the same time, it's crucial to monitor both the other person's and our own body language, quickly correcting any signs of closed-off behavior like crossed arms or inappropriate facial expressions.

It may sound simple, but this final step is often overlooked, even by those who are aware of its importance. Sometimes, after a consulting session with a company, the company's administrator will send me a snapshot from one of the workshops: the room was packed, behind me was a large photograph of the planet on a blue background, and I was standing in front of the team, facing the person who was speaking at that moment. It was a beautiful image, except that when I saw it (meaning when I saw myself), I also saw those closed-off attitudes that I had just advised to avoid: my arms were crossed, my feet were crossed, and I was biting my lower lip. When I saw the photo, I instantly remembered the discomfort I had felt. The person at the microphone was completely uninterested in engaging with their team and was just rambling on in an endless monologue. "How can you build a team if you ignore those in front of you?" I wondered at that time. "Don't you realize that no one has been listening to you for a while?" That snapshot unequivocally proves that no matter how much we try to be careful and keep our emotions under control, they can slip away, and it only takes a second for someone to notice them (in my case, the camera of an iPhone).

To prevent that from happening, we must remember to step back from the scene we are in. Regarding team building, the speaker should have paid more attention to their team. Once I realized that something was not working in the speaker's approach, I should have interrupted the monologue with any excuse and helped them regain control of their audience.

Once we have established that we need to focus on the other person without neglecting to monitor our nonverbal communication (in essence, just refraining from doing what both parties in the described event did), we need to move on to HOW to focus on the other person. Our nonverbal language is essential, but it alone will not be enough to make us genuinely receptive, meaning able to listen.

We should listen not just to respond but to truly understand the other person's motivations: what drives them to be who they are, to say what they say, to seek us as a connection, to look beyond the words and comprehend their origin. We are not seeking consensus to receive or give. Still, we need to understand the other person to categorize the information and evaluate the relationship we can build with them. It is undoubtedly more complicated to say than to do.

Essentially, we must listen actively. First and foremost, we must distinguish listening from hearing. Furthermore, they're not the same: hearing is a passive, mechanical process, while listening requires active involvement.

But how do I know if the listening was "active"? And what does active mean? To actively listen, we must not silently attend to the conversation like a spectator but rather listen to the details of what is being shared, connecting the questions we will ask to what is being disclosed.

Therefore, listening to understand through our active participation.

Actively listening is an act of generosity towards our interlocutor.

We listen with generosity.

We generously ask for further clarification.

Generously, we share what we feel, think, and find beneficial to the conversation.

We utilize what we have listened to and received to reach the other person, understand how we can be of assistance, and create a lasting relationship.

To determine if we have been effective in this operation, we must ask ourselves: "How much do I know about the other person, and how much do they know about me?"

The rule states that we should always know more.

Why?

Because the information we have gathered about the desires, aspirations, family, school, work, pets, problems, or joys of the person we have listened to will serve as inspiration for our following conversation, which will show our new contact that we are interested in them and their life, beyond mere connection and business.

A moment will usually come, either towards the end of the second meeting or at the beginning of the third, when the other person will say to you, "Tell me more about yourself. It feels like we've known each other forever, but I know so little about you."

I'd bet money on it.

It always happens.

This is a sign that our listening has been effective. Building this connection structure, starting with empathy and going through active listening, is a communicative path to making a positive relationship.

#3. PREPARATION

We attended a networking event and met several people who could be valuable contacts for us. First impressions are made at events like these; those initial connections could turn into business partnerships or collaborations.

The first thing we will do once we get home is go on LinkedIn and request a connection with that contact. We can send a message referring to something we discussed at the event: "It was a pleasure meeting you today, and your work in naval engineering deserves further exploration. Can we have a virtual coffee? Let me know when you're available."

We've set up a meeting with a contact who could be beneficial for our career or business.

Now, we need to research that specific person to better understand who we're talking to. I generally advise against connecting on personal social media platforms like Facebook and recommend sticking to professional networks like LinkedIn, which has a global reach, or region-specific platforms like Xing if you're in Germany.

Looking at personal profiles helps me understand someone's interests, political and religious views, and preferences. People share everything, and every piece of information can guide future conversations toward a positive outcome. It is always advisable to avoid sharing your political opinions, especially if you realize that you and your conversation partner hold opposing views. Getting into such a conversation doesn't benefit anyone, as the old Latin saying goes, 'CUI PRODEST?' (Who benefits?).

So, preparing for the meeting is beneficial as it helps us avoid any pitfalls and stick to smoother paths.

#4. ASSERTIVE

When it comes to communication, the common belief is that the most essential part is the choice of words spoken. However, it's fourth on the list of suggestions I'm giving you. Once we have created an empathetic environment, actively listened, and laid the groundwork for a positive and smooth interaction, we must consider the type of communication and the selection of the right words, which are closely connected to the desired outcome of the interaction.

How do we go about it?

Let's start by establishing the "*why.*"

Why are we meeting that person? What common interests do we have? How could we be mutually valuable? Or how can we be of help to them? Once we understand the purpose of the meeting, we should focus on simulating the conversation. Where will this conversation lead, or rather, what outcome do we hope to achieve? The *predictable result* is a simple map that will guide us in structuring a positive relationship, starting from the first encounter and the first impression.

Here's what it's about: building strong points within what we are seeking, what we want, and what we hope will happen. We need to be confident in what we bring to the table and approach the conversation armed with key tools like active listening and effective communication to achieve our goals.

The communication technique I apply and teach is related to assertiveness. There's no easy way to put it—whether you call it effective communication, speaking your mind, or being straightforward.

Definition: Assertive communication allows you to listen to others without giving up on expressing your thoughts.

We are not talking about Marshall Rosenberg's Giraffe Language when we refer to assertiveness. In 1960, Marshall Rosenberg developed a communication process aimed at finding greater authenticity, understanding, deeper connections, and conflict resolution. According to Marshall Rosenberg, the language we use and how we use words play a crucial role in staying empathetically connected to ourselves and others.

Giraffe Communication is Nonviolent Communication based on

three aspects:
1. Self-empathy, listening to oneself
2. Empathy, listening to others
3. Honest self-expression, authentically expressing one's feelings and needs.

It's a four-step communication process that helps us understand what's going on within ourselves and others, providing clarity[33] through:
1. Observation of facts
2. Observation of feelings
3. Observation of needs
4. Observation of requests

While Giraffe Language is the essence of nonviolent communication, assertiveness is more closely related to "radical candor" because it does not exclude conflict when necessary or functional. The cornerstone of assertiveness is setting *our own non-negotiable terms*—things we'd never give up, no matter what. It involves creating a defensive structure around our clear, well-defined self and non-negotiables. "I will never give up on expressing what I feel," "I will never avoid negative people or situations," "I will never stop spending time with my friends at least once a week/month," "I will never give up on dedicating time to my family," "I will never stop working," "I will never give up on pursuing my dreams," etc.

Once we have established our foundations, we are ready to talk to the other person. Speaking also means actively listening. So always and consistently listen (not just hear!) to the other person before expressing ourselves. This way, we build empathy and gather valuable information to lay the groundwork for this new beneficial relationship.

Then, when it is our turn, we will know what to say and how to say it.

ALWAYS THINK ABOUT THE CONSEQUENCES!

---

[33] https://www.villaggioempatico.it/comunicazione-nonviolenta

It's crucial to think ahead about the impact of what we're going to say. We must always try to predict the other person's reaction as much as possible to express ourselves freely. As mentioned earlier, we cannot control what others will say, but we can control what we say. This is not trivial if we consider that anything we say will lead to a reaction. We must be prepared to face the consequences that will follow our words.

You can learn a variety of communication techniques to improve interactions with colleagues, family, friends, and significant others. However, this book is not intended as a how-to manual; it is simply a range of options that unfold before the reader's eyes. The critical realization is that it can be done and learned It's better to go on this journey prepared. As self-taught individuals, it takes a lifetime of change, all geared toward a passion for communication and building relationships.

#5. CARE

No matter why we started building a valuable network, it's crucial to stay focused on our main goal, which serves as a reminder of why we're doing it.
We are not hunting for a database to sell; we don't want to open a headhunter recruitment office.
The term 'headhunter' serves as a perfect explanation for what I'm getting at in this paragraph.
Headhunter means "hunters of heads" and refers to those who work to identify ideal candidates for specific job positions.
Networking to construct mutually valuable relationships does not involve "hunting." We are not on the hunt.
If we know that one of our connections is nearby, we are the ones who jump on a bus, car, train, or plane to meet that person, even just for a greeting.
While revising this paragraph, I was in the United States for work and study when I heard that a close friend's wife from Mumbai, India, was in Texas. So, after taking my son Antonio to the airport for his flight back to Italy, I decided to hop on a flight to Texas to catch up with my friend and her daughters.

I hadn't seen them since February 2019; usually, I would go to India every year on February 12th for a festival that her family organizes for the entire city of Virar (a beautiful opportunity to learn about Indian culture, so fascinating and deeply respectful of human relationships).

Why fly four hours to Texas just to say hello?

Because the network is fueled by human exchange. Because we take care of the contacts with whom we know we can build something good.

We are not hunters; we are farmers.

Human relationships—or any relationships for that matter—are like plants. If we want them to bear fruit, we must water them, prune them, maybe even give them a name, and talk to them occasionally. Nurturing means feeding both the plant and the relationship with positive energy.

This is who we are: cultivators of positive human relationships.

#6. FUN

The evolution in how we manage our contacts, communicate with them, and connect in a mutually beneficial way cannot ignore the aspect of enjoyment. We have already talked about taming in this regard, but I have one last piece of advice for you as a conclusion to this booklet: have fun while building your network, have fun while nurturing it, and do so whenever possible.

If you're not having fun, find a way to change course. Change course if you don't like the people around you (or you don't want them anymore, or worse, they make you feel bad). If you feel stuck in your job, activities, or commitments, it's time to shake things up. That doesn't necessarily mean you have to drop everything and chase the latest YOLO trend or move halfway around the world. You don't have to quit your job or shut down your business; sometimes, all it takes is a change in perspective to see new opportunities.

About the Author

About the Author
Irene Magistro

In the age of transitory digital encounters, the *Intellectual Stripper* emerges as a beacon of transformation, urging individuals to venture beyond the shallow depths of conventional networking. This masterful workbook beckons its readers to shed their societal masks and biases, championing the cultivation of genuine, impactful connections. Delve into the diverse phases of networking, tackle cognitive biases head-on, and set forth on a journey to create sustainable connections rooted in authenticity and shared purpose.

About the Author:

Irene Magistro, more than just an author, is a visionary in the realm of networking. While the traditional accolades and certifications speak to their prowess, it's their profound passion and dedication that truly sets them apart. A proud collaborator with a renowned Leadership program in the U.S., Irene has not only honed their networking prowess but has also empowered over a thousand global individuals, subsequently establishing an impressive worldwide network.

Beyond the traditional confines of networking, Irene is dedicated to the growth and nurturing of talent networks, fostering a rich environment of engagement, mutual support, and collaboration. Their commitment extends into the realm of "rainmaking," aiding businesses and professionals in amplifying their international connectivity. This dedication is supplemented by their expertise in cross-cultural communication, prepping entrepreneurs and professionals for global triumphs.

However, *Intellectual Stripper* is not just a book. It's Irene's tangible gift to the world — a manifestation of their commitment to give, to share, and to inspire. At the crux of their philosophy lies the beautiful act of giving, a testament to the essence of genuine human interaction.

Embark on this transformative journey with Irene. Uncover the magic of authentic networking, unlock boundless opportunities, and let's collectively shape a more connected and brighter future. Experience networking like never before, and allow it to revolutionize your world.

End Credits

Title: Intellectual Stripper

Author: Irene Magistro

Cover Design: Canvas Pro

Foreword: Mindy Gibbins-Klein
Founder of The Book Midwife® and author of The Thoughtful Leader

Copyright © 2022 by Irene Magistro

All rights reserved.

No part of this book may be reproduced or transmitted in any form or by any means, electronic or mechanical, including photocopying, recording, or any other information storage and retrieval system, without prior written permission from the publisher.

Published by: Self Published on Amazon

ISBN: 13: 979-8398831047

Printed in USA

For more information, visit our website: www.irenemagistro.com

Disclaimer:

The information and advice provided in this book are intended for general informational purposes only and should not be considered professional or legal advice. The author and publisher disclaim any liability for the use or misuse of any information contained herein. Readers should consult with a professional for any specific networking or intellectual pursuits.

Please recycle this book responsibly.

Printed in Great Britain
by Amazon